THE INFLUENCE OF THE FABIAN COLONIAL BUREAU

ON THE INDEPENDENCE MOVEMENT IN TANGANYIKA

THE INFLUENCE OF THE FABIAN COLONIAL BUREAU

ON THE INDEPENDENCE MOVEMENT IN TANGANYIKA

BY

DANIEL R. SMITH

OHIO UNIVERSITY
CENTER FOR INTERNATIONAL STUDIES
MONOGRAPHS IN INTERNATIONAL STUDIES

AFRICA SERIES NUMBER 44
Athens, Ohio 1985

Library of Congress Cataloging in Publication Data
Smith, Daniel R.
   The influence of the Fabian Colonial Bureau on
the independence movement in Tanganyika.

   (Monographs in international studies. Africa
series ; no. 44)
   Bibliography: p.
   1. Tanganyika--Politics and government. 2. National
liberation movements--Tanganyika. 3. Fabian Colonial
Bureau. I. Title. II. Series.
DT447.S6 1984   967.8'2'03   84-18959
ISBN 0-89680-125-X

ISBN: 0-89680-125-X

BIOGRAPHICAL SKETCH

Daniel R. Smith holds the rank of Associate Professor in the Department of History and Political Science at Iona College, New Rochelle, New York. His major areas of teaching interest include: Contemporary Africa and Comparative Non-Western Political Systems.

Professor Smith received his Ph.D. in African History from St. John's University in 1974. His present research interest is focused upon the process of decolonization in British East Africa.

He is a resident of Bronxville, New York.

CONTENTS

PREFACE

In the period 1945 - 1961 the trust territory of Tanganyika became the site of a protracted conflict which pitted the British government against the African nationalist movement led by Julius Nyerere. The controversy centered upon the questions of the speed with which the trusteeship would be granted independence and the nature of the constitutional changes to be adopted to achieve that goal. The British Colonial Office was insistent that the evolutionary process towards self-rule had to involve a slow, well supervised alteration and was adamant in its position that once independence was attained political and economic safeguards would have to be provided for the non-African elements of Tanganyika's population. At the opposite extreme, the African nationalists insisted upon a rapid transition toward independence and called for the incorporation of a number of policies which would guarantee black majority rule.

The conflict between these two factions was complicated by Tanganyika's status as a trusteeship. Since the territory was legally under the control of the United Nations Trusteeship Council any compromises made between the Crown and the nationalists were subject to review by the international body. The fact that the Council itself was splintered into two ideological factions, which pitted the Western powers against both the Communist bloc states and the recently liberated nations of the Third World added additional elements of tension and confusion to the debate concerning Tanganyika's future.

During the period under study all of the competing groups noted above came under the influence of the Fabian Colonial Bureau. The Fabians were unquestionably sympathetic to the goals of the nationalists and provided the African leaders with advice, favorable publicity and support via their contacts within the British government and at the United Nations throughout the course of the independence movement. At the same time, however, the Fabian Bureau endorsed the policies of the British Colonial Office on those occasions when it believed that the Crown proposals offered the most reasonable solution to a particular territorial problem.

The purpose of this study is to demonstrate that the Fabian Colonial Bureau, by consistently maintaining a position that offered a balanced and reasonable approach to the political evolution of Tanganyika, was able to use its influence within the home government and its contacts with key African political organizations within the trusteeship to help formulate a series of viable compromises on the questions of the pace and structure of the territory's development towards independence. The author hopes to demonstrate that, throughout the period under study, the Fabian Colonial Bureau consistently offered well-developed, rational and balanced plans for the trusteeship's political evolution. These were of great value in a potentially explosive situation, during which the other interest groups involved often endorsed plans for the territory that could be classified as less than equitable to all parties concerned.

The bulk of the primary source material utilized in this study was obtained from an examination of the manuscripts available in the Rhodes House Africana collection at Oxford University. Key documents utilized from that source include the complete papers of the Fabian Colonial Bureau and the personal memoirs of numerous British administrators stationed in Tanganyika. Additional research was undertaken at the headquarters of both the Conservative and Labour parties in London and at the Institute for Commonwealth Studies at Oxford. Valuable supplementary information was obtained from the African collections at Boston, Syracuse and Northwestern Universities.

CHAPTER I

BACKGROUND TO THE CONFLICT

The Territory and Its People

Tanganyika officially came under British rule on July 22, 1922 when the League of Nations agreed that the territory formerly known as German East Africa would be administered by the Crown as a mandate for the international organization. At the close of World War Two, the territory was transferred to the control of the United Nations Trusteeship Council with Great Britain designated as the "Administering Authority."

Tanganyika was a vast but resource poor area. The only viable source of economic activity involved the production of sisal, cotton and tobacco which were raised for export, primarily to Great Britain.

The population of Tanganyika was divided into three racial groups; African, Asian and European. The Africans, who represented some 98% of the territory's population were separated into over 120 tribal groups. Tanganyika also possessed an Asian population who were divided into a number of Indian, Pakastani, Goan, and Arab communities and who accounted for less than 1% of the total population. Europeans in the territory represented over 30 different nationalities and were roughly equal in size to the Asian groups. The population of Tanganyika was 9,238,000 by independence. The proportion of the population represented by each of the three racial groups remained essentially the same throughout the period under study.

The vast majority of the African population were subsistence level farmers who raised crops on scattered homesteads located in isolated rural areas. Throughout the colonial period, fewer than 10% of the total black population were regular wage earners and even fewer were formally educated.

The Asian communities occupied a middle position in Tanganyikan society. Members of this ethnic group were concentrated in Dar es Salaam and in the larger towns, where they were employed in the wholesale and retail trades, commercial banking, and the civil service.

The European component of the population consisted of government administrators, civil servants, plantation owners, missionaries, and businessmen. The vast majority of all high level civil servants and colonial administrators were Europeans.

1

Political Background

In 1926 a critical period of Tanganyikan political development began. It was then that Sir Donald Cameron introduced the concept of "indirect rule" into the territorial administration. Under this system, the major internal and external affairs of the territory were controlled by the colonial administrative staff and the British home government. On the local level, administration in the interior of Tanganyika was placed in the hands of traditional indigenous rulers, referred to as the "native authorities." Beside fulfilling their traditional leadership functions, the local leaders were required to perform certain administrative tasks for the colonial government. Included among these were the levying and collecting of taxes, maintenance of law and order and the enforcement of social welfare and local development projects.

While indirect rule was theoretically supposed to produce gradual alterations in traditional societies to prepare them for modern political participation, in reality the Crown accomplished little more than to maintain law and order in the African territories in which this system was practiced. Once given official sanction by the colonial administration, most traditional leaders tended to jealously guard their authority and to resist any attempt aimed at evolving democratic systems of representation.

Administrative Framework

The head of the colonial administration in Tanganyika was the Governor. His principal powers included the right to issue ordinances, to appoint official and unofficial members of the Executive and Legislative Councils[1] and to review bills proposed by the legislature.

The Tanganyika Executive Council was created in 1920 as a consultative body to advise the Governor in the formulation of territorial policy. Executive Council members were almost exclusively officials in the Colonial Service, although unofficials were technically admissible to its ranks.

The Tanganyika Legislative Council was established in 1926 and consisted of the Governor, the members of the Executive Council as ex officio members and a designated number of both official and unofficial members, all appointed by the Governor. Thus, the Legislative Council was neither elective nor representative. With the official side of the council possessing a majority, the legislative branch of government could really not serve as a counterforce to the authority of the administration.

2

The territory of Tanganyika was partitioned into eight provinces, each of which was subdivided into districts. The head of each province was the Provincial Commissioner who was responsible for the maintenance of law and order, tax collection, internal improvements, control of the police force and supervision of the local courts in his domain. District Commissioners were responsible for similar duties in their regions.

The Nature of the Trusteeship Agreement

The basic obligations accepted by Great Britain when it transferred Tanganyika from the Mandate system to the Trusteeship system after World War II were to develop free political institutions and to foster participation in these by the indigenous population who, it was understood, would ultimately gain control of the government. However, no provision was made to control the methods employed by the Administering Authority in reaching these objectives. Britain alone was in a position to determine the rate at which the advancement toward self-government would take place and to decide the actual structure of the political system that was evolving in Tanganyika.

Under the stipulations of Article 87 of the U.N. Charter, the Trusteeship Council was empowered to oversee the evolution of Tanganyika toward self-government. It was the responsibility of the Council to examine all reports by the Administering Authority and all petitions received from residents of the Trusteeship. These documents were debated by the Council which then made written observations and recommendations in the form of resolutions, based on a majority vote by the Council members.

The Trusteeship Council was obligated to send periodic "Visiting Missions" to each of the trust territories. These visits, designed to provide the Trusteeship Council with first-hand information gathered by its own members, began in 1948. The trusteeship missions toured Tanganyika every three years until 1960. Mission members would interview colonial officials, local political leaders and private citizens and would accept delegations and petitions from the resident population. Each mission was required to draw up a detailed report of its observations and conclusions which was submitted to the Trusteeship Council. The Council would debate this report and issue its own conclusions which would be forwarded to the Administering Authority.

The Genesis of the Liberal Reform Movement

During the Second World War it became apparent to the British government that the changes produced in her dependencies as a result of the war effort, coupled with a major shift in world public opinion concerning the desirability and justification of maintaining an empire were producing a trend away from imperialism and toward self-rule. As a result, the Crown began to accelerate the pace of development within its territories, recognizing that most dependent areas would ultimately be at least internally self-governing.

However, the home government was divided into two rival factions, each of which possessed its own concept of both the pace at which such developmental programs should be introduced into the colonies and of what constituted a suitable structure of government, once self-rule was attained. The Conservative Party on one hand maintained that the system of indirect rule would have to be preserved and that guarantees concerning the rights of the Asian and European communities would have to be provided, if moderate and well balanced political systems were to emerge in the British dependencies. The conservatives repeatedly stressed the necessity of preceding political change with substantial social, economic and educational development to be introduced over the period of several generations. Liberal activists by contrast (generally affiliated with the Labour Party), insisted upon a rapid acceleration of the political systems within the African dependencies, even if such advances exceeded the pace of social, economic, and educational development. They contended that only immediate and direct exposure to modern political processes would truly prepare Africans for self-rule.

Undoubtedly, the most influential and prestigious of the liberal activist groups to be found in Great Britain was the Fabian Colonial Bureau. This organization was founded in October, 1940, by Labour M.P. Arthur Creech-Jones and the British socialist leaders Rita Hinden, James Betts, and Marjorie Nicholson, as an extension of the Fabian Society. The Bureau's purpose was to collect and coordinate information concerning activities in the dependencies and to foster popular demand within the home government for the dissolution of the Empire. As a branch of the British Fabian Society, the Bureau operated as a progressive reform group dedicated to the gradual spread of world socialism. With particular reference to the British dependencies, Fabians sought to end the traditional concept of an empire based on mercantilism and in its place to create a Commonwealth of freely partici-pating states. Primary among the socialist aspirations was

the plan to introduce a series of long range economic and
social reforms which would distribute the goods and services
of the British Commonwealth among its inhabitants on a more
equitable basis. The Bureau believed that a rapid pace of
political development coupled with substantial economic aid
from the home government was needed to start the dependencies
on the road to self-rule. Fabians contended that political
self-determination, based on rule by the indigenous population of each territory was essential if racial tension which
could undermine the planned Commonwealth of freely partici-
pating states was to be avoided. The Fabian Bureau therefore
dedicated itself to cooperation with emerging nationalist
groups throughout the British Empire. Key among its efforts
was its campaign aimed at educating the British public in
territorial affairs in order to foster a spirit of popular
support within the home government for the liberation movements.[2]

One of the major tasks of the Bureau was to coordinate
the efforts of members of Parliament sympathetic to the
cause of colonial emancipation. The Fabians extensively
researched controversial colonial issues and forwarded the
results to their Parliamentary allies. One of the standard
tactics employed by the Bureau was to prepare a list of
questions for M.P.s to ask in the House of Commons, in order
to solicit information concerning government policy and to
promote public interest in colonial affairs. As the Bureau
expanded its operations, it began to tutor members of
Parliament who expressed a special interest in a given
dependency in an attempt to make them quasi-experts on some
aspect of that territory's colonial situation. By 1955 the
Fabians had twelve members of Commons who concentrated on
issues involving Tanganyika.[3]

The Fabians were by no means the only liberal organiza-
tion concerned with colonial questions. During and immedi-
ately after the Second World War scores of activist groups
sprang to life in Great Britain. Key among these associa-
tions were: the Union of Democratic Control, the Women's
International League for Peace and Freedom, the London Race
Relations Group, the Aborigines Protection Society, the
Racial Unity Movement, the Women's Commonwealth League, the
League of Colonial Peoples, St. Joan's Alliance, the African
Bureau, the Anti-Slavery Society and the Friends of Africa.
All of these organizations shared as a common goal the
termination of colonial rule and the transformation of the
Empire into a Commonwealth. These liberal groups produced a
continuous stream of inexpensive pamphlets and newsletters
aimed at making their views on colonial affairs well-known
to the British public.

During World War Two, Labour Party members of Parliament, encouraged by the liberal activists, began to bring the issue of British colonial policy in Tanganyika to the forefront of debate in the House of Commons. Between 1940 and 1945 Dr. Rita Hinden, Secretary of the Fabian Colonial Bureau, corresponded continually with E. Harvey, a Labour M.P. At her encouragement Harvey initiated a campaign of insistent questioning to gain information concerning the scope of the planned government aid for the fledgling native coffee cooperatives in the territory. It was the Bureau's belief that such indigenous organizations could form the basis of a program of economic amelioration for the African inhabitants. At the same time, R. Sorensen, M.P., plagued the Secretary of State for a guarantee that permanent white settlement in Tanganyika would not be encouraged at the expense of the African population, via the practice of land alienation. In February, 1944, Harvey protested against the use of forced labor in the more isolated sections of the territory and the lack of effort on the part of the colonial government to improve economic and social conditions for black residents. He later called for a Parliamentary examination of working conditions within the trusteeship and for a study to determine what steps could be taken to raise the African standard of living. Finally, during these years the Fabian Colonial Bureau conducted an investigation into the use of black conscript labor on sisal and rubber planations in Tanganyika.

Thus, by 1945, the Fabian Bureau had established a well organized and influential pressure group, dedicated to the protection of African interests in Tanganyika. Although the socialists recognized that Britain was ultimately prepared to free the trusteeship, they were not satisfied with the Crown's nebulous plans for territorial advancement. Rather, they called for a concentrated effort to ameliorate conditions within the territory as soon as possible and for the initiation of immediate programs of modern political development. Writing to M.P. Arthur Creech-Jones (who later became Secretary of State for the Colonies) Rita Hinden remarked:

> The general limitation of colonial policy as we know it at the moment, that is to say, Trusteeship leading to self-government, is a vague undefined future, combined with the Colonial Development and Welfare Act. It seems to me that neither this political concept nor this economic concept is sufficient to meet the needs of today...
> The whole position in Eastern and Central Africa demands a much bolder treatment than the

present policy, either economic and political, can offer.[4]

Accordingly, by the end of the Second World War, Great Britain stood prepared to make gradual but major changes in her colonial policies by slowly evolving her subject people toward self-government. At the same time, there existed within Britain an active socialist movement dedicated to a pace of colonial development toward independence which was far more rapid than that planned by the home government. By 1945 the Fabian Colonial Bureau had taken a special interest in the territory of Tanganyika and had begun to probe official policies which it suspected of not always serving the best interests of the African population.

CHAPTER II

THE BEGINNINGS OF FABIAN INVOLVEMENT: 1945-50

Territorial Developments

It was the British government itself which took the first steps to initiate widesweeping political, economic, and social changes within Tanganyika. In 1945 general elections in Great Britain brought the Labour Party into power. The new regime, which was comprised of the more liberal elements of the home government, quickly formulated plans to increase the pace of political evolution within the dependencies. Most significantly, in that year Arthur Creech-Jones assumed the post of Secretary of State for the Colonies.[5] From 1940 to 1945 Jones had served as Chairman of the Fabian Colonial Bureau. Upon his assumption of the top post in the British Colonial Office, the socialists in Britain acquired a direct contact with Downing Street.

Under Jones' leadership the pace of development in the colonies accelerated rapidly, thus giving the fledgling nationalist movements ample opportunity to grow. The new Secretary of State's attitude concerning political development is reflected in his April, 1946, address to the General Meeting of the Labour Party:

> We have entered into a phase of Colonial history in which there is a widespread demand from the colonial peoples, or at any rate from the more vocal elements, for more practical evidence of the sincerity of our government on the colonial issues.
>
> I am convinced that in this modern age with its forces of nationalism and freedom, with the spread of educational and economic changes and the political and social awakening going on, we must adjust ourselves to a much quicker tempo of constitutional development than would have seemed practicable a few years ago. We have to experiment boldly though not necessarily rashly and to recognize that while the transfer of power to people not fully trained or with adequate experience or tradition to exercise it will lead to mistakes being made, it is only through actual experience in the exercises of responsibility that people can acquire a sense of duty and service.
>
> The process may be a painful one but the alternatives of increasing bitterness and tension in the relations of the people to the government would be disasterous.[6]

9

Although the ultimate goal of its colonial policy was clear, the Labour Party was faced with a dilemma. On the other hand, it was committed to advance the pace of political development in the territories as rapidly as possible. At the same time, however, it had to insure that the economic and social institutions of each territory were sufficiently advanced by independence to meet the demands of a modern society. Maintenance of the delicate balance between these two aspects of development was to become a major problem for the Labour regime.[7]

With specific reference to Tanganyika, one of the most pressing problems to be addressed by the new Labour government was the question of the effectiveness of indirect rule. It was clear that throughout the territory native authorities were using the system to entrench their base of traditional control rather than to gradually introduce popular participation in the decision-making process. The growing pool of westernized Africans were especially resentful of the inadequacies of the system. By 1950 none other than Lord Hailey had warned that unless a method were found for admitting the educated elite and progressive young Africans into the local political process, the indirect rule system would end in total failure.[8]

In response to this problem, in the 1945-50 period, Great Britain formulated the policy known as the "multiracial" or "partnership" system. This new approach was designed to afford westernized Africans an opportunity to participate in modern political, economic, and social developments and yet at the same time to safeguard the interests of the European and Asian communities. Under this new system, separate administrative and social services were provided for each of the three races in Tanganyika.

In theory, "partnership" was designed to permit each community to develop its own potential as fully as possible and to contribute to the development of the territory in accordance to its ability. In reality, the policy guaranteed the preservation of privileged positions in Tanganyikan society for the members of the Asian and European communities.

In an effort to foster the systems of indirect rule and partnership the British government initiated a series of political changes within Tanganyika. In December, 1945, the first two Africans were appointed to the Legislative Council. Notably, both were native administrators rather than members of the modern elite. On November 23, 1949, Sir Edward Twining, the newly appointed Governor, announced a series of local political reforms. Key among these was a plan to create a number of provincial councils, each based on inter-racial and inter-tribal lines, to serve as a link between traditional authorities, modern political activists, and the administration. At some undesignated point in the future the provincial councils would be evolved into a territorial body.

On December 12, 1949, the Governor introduced the most important innovation for political advancement of the 1945-50 period; the establishment of a committee to study the question of constitutional evolution. No sooner had the committee been formed, than it was sent a memorandum by the Governor suggesting the creation of an unofficial majority in the legislature, to be selected through an electoral college system. Electors would be chosen by the recently instituted provincial councils, with one African and one non-African representative selected from each province.

When the Committee released its findings in April, 1951, it was clear that the Twining memorandum had by no means dominated the members' thinking. The Report rejected the proposal for an unofficial majority, stating that far more political experience in representative government would have to precede such a step.[9] The committee recommended an enlargement of the Legislative Council and the establishment of "parity" among its unofficial members.[10] The report also rejected the proposed provincial councils and the electoral college system as both impractical and cumbersome. Finally, it suggested that at least one-third of the allotted African seats on the new Legislative Council be reserved for non-chiefs, to issue the educated elite more opportunity for political participation.

During this period, the Colonial Office also began to introduce a series of economic development schemes in the trusteeship. In 1946 a Ten-Year Development and Welfare Program began operation. By 1950, some 24 million pounds had been expended for the improvement of Tanganyika's trans-portation, communication and educational facilities. Especially heavy stress was placed on agricultural experi-mentation.

In order to support its efforts at economic growth, the Colonial Office initiated a plan to recruit new white settlers into the area. It was felt that additional European immigration was needed to provide Tanganyika with a pool of prosperous agriculturalists sufficient to prime the sagging post-war economy. Part of this recruitment effort included the initiation of the ill-fated Groundnut Scheme, which proved to be one of the major fiascos of Britain's post-war colonial development efforts. A key element of this project

11

was the plan to "alienate" vast tracts of land for future white settlement.[11]

The final major segment of the Administering Authority's attempts to develop the territory consisted of the initiation of a number of compulsory programs designed to improve agricultural productivity. The territory's Ten-Year Plan included over forty such schemes, aimed at preventing soil erosion, increasing crop yield and improving livestock utilization.

However, the use of such modern agricultural methods such as tie-ridging, cattle-culling, destocking, innoculation, and cattle-dipping, as well as the concept of using chemicals for soil improvement were misunderstood by many Africans and consequently were viewed as threats to the traditional way of life.

Territorial Political Activism: 1945-50

In the period 1945-50 the first significant indigenous political associations were beginning to emerge in Tanganyika. Most of these early organizations shared certain characteristics. All limited their activities to complaints and petitions through official channels. All possessed a modest following and restricted their aims to the solution of specific parochial issues.

Unquestionably the most active of the early political organizations was the Tanganyika African Association (T.A.A.) which was founded in Dar es Salaam in 1927 with the help of colonial administrators who wished to create a legitimate and controllable forum for African political activity. Because of its close association with the government, in its early years the T.A.A. limited its political operation to the holding of public debates to shed light on controversial issues. The Association was nonetheless the most modern and best organized of all the early political activist groups. T.A.A. was open to all Africans and established several branch offices throughout the territory. Most of its early members were teachers or civil servants.

As African political involvement assumed a more unified form, the white settler community of Tanganyika began to take a much greater interest in territorial affairs. Throughout the independence drive the European settlers revealed themselves as a highly conservative group, who were strongly opposed to the idea of increased African political activity. Consequently, any suggestions by liberal reformers aimed at increasing African control were condemned by the white community as radical and subversive. Noting this attitude, one educated African remarked:

12

...Socialists and people with socialist connections tend to be labelled "Communists" here. In fact, it would appear that the greater bulk of Europeans, both officials and non-officials out here, to say the least, have no respect for liberal reformers.[12]

White settlers were especially interested in the question of land alienation. Under the Cameron administration, land tenure leases had been limited to thirty-three year periods, while customary tenure in other East and Central African territories was based on ninety-nine year contracts. Settlers continuously protested the Tanganyikan policy and cited it as the main cause of the territory's failure to encourage substantial European immigration.

The Tanganyika European Council, which was the most active of the early white settler groups, was founded in October, 1950. The Council centered its political program on the demand for the election of Asian and European representatives to the Legislative Council based on communal rolls.[13] It also called for the introduction of a highly qualitative franchise which would clearly favor members of the European community.

While Europeans and Africans were founding their first significant political associations, the Asian community tended to avoid involvement in controversial issues. The one exception to this isolationalist tendency in the early post-war years was the Central Moslem Association, many of whose members maintained close contact with the Fabian Colonial Bureau. In July 1950 the organization held a special meeting in Dar es Salaam to consider the question of future political developments. There it passed a resolution stating:

> ...any racial or colour division...of the population such as European or Asian or African is repugnant to our faith and injurious to our interests...we recommend that a common roll of franchise be adopted for all permanent residents of Tanganyika as 'Tanganyikans' without any distinctions whatsoever.[14]

Clearly then, even as early as the 1945-50 period, serious conflicts of interest and differences in approach to political development separated the three ethnic communities of Tanganyika.

13

The Influence of the United Nations

The debates which arose between 1945 and 1950 concerning the development of Tanganyika were further complicated by the activities of the Trusteeship Council. In the early post-war period, this body became the site of the ideological confrontation between the colonial powers and the anti-imperialist nations.

The types of criticism leveled by members of the international body against Great Britain were much more severe than those raised by dissident factions within the home government. While the British liberals recognized that self-government was imminent and, therefore, limited their objections to issues involving the pace and structure of political evolution, the Soviet Union and her allies on the Trusteeship Council repeatedly charged that Britain had no intention of emancipating her global holdings.

The ideological convictions of the anti-imperialist factions also caused them to ignore the positive improvements produced in the territory by the British administration. Virtually every development program for Tanganyika formulated by the Administering Authority from 1945 to 1950 was condemned as either too weak or as a veiled attempt at neo-colonialism.

The first major controversy within the international organization was incited by the activities of the 1948 Visiting Mission. The team encouraged Tanganyikan Africans to openly articulate their opinions concerning the British administration via the use of petitions. The two most significant documents received were those presented by the Dar es Salaam and Shinyanga branches of the T.A.A. Both called for a major program of educational development to bring Africans into the cash economy and to prepare them for political participation. The petitions also called for increased African representation on the Legislative Council, for freedom of speech and press, and for an end to racial discrimination. Interviews with individual Africans throughout the territory revealed an almost universal desire among the elite for similar types of reforms.[15]

The conclusions of the Visiting Mission team were published in 1949. The document was highly critical of the administrations' activites in the area of political development. It especially condemned the absence of a clear plan for evolution toward self-government. The report was also critical of the multi-racial system and of the policy of political advancement via indirect rule. The document stressed that since African members of the Legislative Council were appointed and not elected, there were in reality

14

no spokesmen for indigenous opinion at the central government level. It also claimed that the recently created provincial councils were both ineffective and undemocratic. Most significantly, the U. N. report supported demands made by the T.A.A. for increased African representation on the Legislative Council and for non-racial elections in the near future.

The report was also critical of Britain's economic policies and urged that European immigration be curtailed to protect the interests of the African majority.

The Role of the Fabian Colonial Bureau: 1945-50

As the Second World War was drawing to an end, both the liberal and conservative factions within the home government accepted the fact that the time was at hand for the initiation of the first steps of political advancement which would ultimately bring self-rule to most of Great Britain's dependencies. However, many British liberal organizations, key among which was the Fabian Socialists, were dissatisfied with both the pace at which the colonies were evolving towards self-rule and with the proposed structures of government planned for the dependent areas.

Socialist concern over the future of Tanganyika dated back to the early post-war period. In 1945, the Secretary of the Fabian Colonial Bureau remarked:

> ...the whole question of Tanganyika is very much in the forefront of our minds...we have met a number of people coming from Tanganyika and all reports they bring lead us to feel very anxious about the future of this territory. Its status as a mandate will bring it to the fore when colonial questions are settled at the Peace Conference, following on the proposal for the formation of the new Trusteeship Council at San Francisco. We have therefore been considering preparing some documents for publication on the special question of Tanganyika, and in view of this I have been gathering up many valuable papers and letters which have come my way.[16]

In that year the Fabian Bureau undertook an extensive study of the territory and enlisted the aid of liberal members of Parliament who raised questions in the House of Commons concerning virtually all aspects of the territory's development.[17] The liberals anticipated that the major controversies that would arise in the territory in the early

15

post-war years would center upon the related issues of land tenure and white settlement, the methods and goals of the Overseas Food and Colonial Development corporations and the debate within the Trusteeship Council over the pace and structure of political evolution.[18]

The socialists were convinced that all of these troublesome questions were the product of the tri-racial policy of the Administering Authority. The Fabians demanded that the Colonial Office abandon the system of partnership and in its place formulate a definite, clearly-stated policy towards Tanganyika, based on a guarantee of self-government via democratic processes. One of their basic complaints was that although Britain planned to emancipate her colonies, the process was being retarded by influential interest groups who sought to preserve the Empire for as long as possible. Within Tanganyika, the white settler organizations were viewed as the chief source of such an effort. Fabian Secretary Hinden noted:

> What is really lacking in Tanganyika is obvious--a clear and determined policy. London has stuck to its fundamental ideas that the African should come first, that he should be encouraged toward self-government, that his standard of living should be raised. Once these principles reach Tanganyika they collide with the powerful claims of the minorities and special interests on the spot. In a hundred insidious ways Colonial Office policy is watered down by local pressures; and who is there, other than the harried official, to combat the subtle influence on his doorstep of employers, companies, planters and settlers? The Africans are unorganized, uneducated, politically untrained; the Indians are caught precariously between the upper Europeans and lower African millstones, and are aware of their own unpopularity. The whole psychology of Tanganyikan politics is wrong, and no amount of white self-righteousness or black resentment can set it right. Only an absolutely unequivocal policy can break through the confusion.[19]

The demand of the Fabian Colonial Bureau for rapid territorial development led to open conflict in Parliament between the supporters of colonial emancipation and those who sought to preserve the Empire. This dissension was manifested in many forms and involved multifold issues. In January, 1945, Lord Ammon, at the urging of Rita Hinden, publicized a demand that Africans in Tanganyika be trained for administrative positions in government. When the Colonial Office admitted that few steps had been taken in this direction, Ammon concluded that "...this is a side of the question of Colonial Government which requires attention and insistent pressuring on the Colonial Office".[20] In the same year, Labour M.P. John Dugdale demanded a Parliamentary inquiry to determine why African wages in urban areas were so low that blacks were prevented from living within the townships and consequently were denied exposure to modern influences.[21] A follow up report by the Labour party advisor to the Colonial Office, Major Orde Browne, revealed that significantly substandard wages and working conditions for African laborers were to be found throughout the territory. The report also revealed that the administration was not fulfilling its legal obligations to supply housing and adequate health facilities to black government employees.[22] The entire issue was subsequently raised in the House of Commons by Member A. B. Bottomly at the urging of the Fabian Bureau.

The debate soon extended to the House of Lords, where it was further revealed that Tanganyikan blacks were subject to penal sanctions for breaking contracts, that forced recruitment tactics were employed by the native authorities and that mass corporal punishment was commonplace in many isolated regions of the trusteeship.[23]

The Overseas Food Corporation and the Groundnut Scheme were also major sources of conflict within the home government. When the Fabians discovered that European personnel working on the scheme often became permanent settlers upon the termination of their contracts and that even temporary resident employees were becoming involved in white settler politics, they demanded a fullscale investigation. This in turn led to a series of heated Parliamentary debates.[24]

Throughout this period, there were also several major controversies concerning economic development policies in Tanganyika which divided the liberal and conservative elements of the home government. Key among these issues was the question of further white settlement. The Labour Party and the liberal reform groups were adamantly opposed to additional white immigration. They insisted that increased European settlement inevitably resulted in special economic concessions for whites, such as agricultural subsidies and price controlling, domination of the representative organs of government and special land acquisition privileges.

Conservatives, on the other hand, contended that increased white settlement should be supported not merely because it provided an economic opportunity for Europeans but because it brought to the dependency the pool of experienced entrepreneurs needed to develop it. A major victory in this area was achieved by the conservative forces in February, 1949. The report of the 1948 Visiting Mission was released at that time and suggested the curtailment of European settlement. In response to Conservative demands for a refutation of this proposal, Secretary of State Creech-Jones announced:

> His Majesty's Government are prepared to agree to schemes for non-African settlement in Tanganyika, on the understanding that the land in question is not required for African occupation, and that the schemes are economically sound. I recognize the value of non-African enterprise and that it must be viewed as an integral part of the development of the Territory as a whole.[25]

This concession by the liberal Secretary of State was based on his belief that the territory could not hope to make any significant economic progress without substantial settler investment. As a result, some 100 Europeans were given land grants in 1949. At no time however, did the Secretary plan to make open settlement a permanent or long range feature of Tanganyika's administrative policy.[26]

In response, liberal elements within Britain launched a campaign to thwart future white settlement. The Fabian Bureau, which led the liberal opposition, petitioned directly to the Secretary of State:

> A major source of trouble is that it is by no means clear what the policy of the Government is on the question of European land settlement in Tanganyika, and Africans are fearful that the history of Kenya is about to repeat itself... the land alienation policies have been criticized time without number in the Labour movement, and it has always been our hope that, with a Labour Government in office, the mistakes of the past would not be repeated in the Colonies neighboring on Kenya. This does not mean to say that we are not aware of the valuable contribution to the <u>economic</u> life of the country made by European capital, skill and enterprise, but we claim that the same contributions could be made without alienating land for settlement... Once European settlement is permitted, the settlers naturally develop a political stake in the country; they put forward claims for

18

privileged treatment and <u>political</u> consequences,
in terms of African resentment outweigh by far the
benefits of an economic order that the settlers
are able to bring.

There are now signs of this unfortunate
sequence of events occurring in Tanganyika, and we
are filled with disquiet by the reports coming
from that country.... It is obvious that immense
pressure is being exerted by Europeans in
Tanganyika to gain possession of more and more
land. They have many more opportunities of voicing
their claims loudly than have the Africans, who--
apart from the Trusteeship Council of the United
Nations -- can look for protection only to you,
Sir, and to your Officials in the Colonial Office
and on the spot, and with all diffidence, express
the hope that you give this problem, with all its
manifold dangers and political implications, your
earnest attention and consider the possiblity of
an unambiguous statement of where, exactly, His
Majesty's Government stands.[27]

Once again however, the liberal forces were to suffer a
setback rendered by one of their own members. In reply to
the Bureau's request the Secretary of State commented:

I can see no reason for varying the policy
regarding European settlement which has been
followed by my predecessors. In a vast country
with a comparatively sparse and scattered population, such as Tanganyika, the cost of administration is inevitably very high. At the same time,
there is urgent need to increase educational and
medical facilities for the African population of
the territory. If this is to be done there must
first be a considerable expansion of the Government's revenues and to secure that we must develop
the economic resources of the territory to the
utmost by all possible means and with the least
possible delay.

...In these circumstances I think your Committee need not fear that the political disadvantage
of the proposed policy of European settlement in
Tanganyika will outweigh the economic and other
advantages which the territory will derive from
it.[28]

While the debate over European immigration was in progress,
a second major liberal-conservative confrontation was taking
place. This involved the question of land alienation. The

dispute commenced in May, 1946, when the Land Settlement Board of Tanganyika proposed that the Member for Lands and Mines be allowed to handle all petitions for grants and that preferential treatment be given to veterans and experienced small scale white farmers. The Fabian Bureau launched a protest in the House of Commons via the cooperation of M. P. Charles Smith. As a result of his insistent protests, the proposition was abandoned.[29]

Later that year, the Post-War Planning Committee which had been created to draw up a blueprint for future territorial development suggested that a Land Settlement Board and Office be established to study the possibility of ninety-nine year leases being granted to new settlers. Again the socialists protested loudly to both the press and the Colonial Office, thus temporarily blocking the measure.[30]

It was during this period that the most controversial land alienation problem in Tanganyikan history had its inception. The issue centered around the government plan to remove about 1,000 members of the Meru tribe from the Sanya corridor, a plateau lying between Mts. Meru and Kilimanjaro, to new lands some forty miles to the west. Although the full storm of controversy over the Meru land case did not break until the 1951-54 period, dissatisfaction with the proposals was expressed by a local elite activist group, the Meru Citizens Union, and by the T.A.A. Both organizations ultimately petitioned the United Nations to block the transfer.

The liberal forces within Great Britain were quick to conduct an investigation into the situation. The Secretary of State was deluged with a constant stream of questions from the socialists concerning the fate of the Meru people and the possible implications of the move in relation to land alienation policies for the territory as a whole. In June, 1950, at the request of the Fabian Colonial Bureau, Michael Parker, a Labour M.P., asked the Secretary of State to guarantee that Tanganyika would not be divided into specified areas for European and African settlement. The Secretary of State assured him that no such a plan was intended by His Majesty's Government. This promise was reinforced in a letter from the Secretary to Rita Hinden in October, 1950:

> ...there is no intention of dividing Tanganyika into native reserves and areas for non-native occupation. Alienated areas are, and will continue to be, scattered among areas of African settlement throughout the Territory.[31]

Although the Colonial Office steadfastly maintained that it had no plan for massive European settlement or land alienation, lack of a clear policy statement produced considerable unrest within the socialist ranks of the home government. It was feared that the policy of deciding land grants and settlement cases on an individual basis could ultimately result in the development of an overly powerful white settler group within Tanganyika.

Perhaps the most heated debate over land policy in the trusteeship during the 1945-50 period began in February, 1950, when the Member for Lands and Mines, publicly stated that the government was planning to alienate one hundred farms of 1,000 acres apiece for future white settlers each year for an indefinite period of time. He further announced that plans were being drawn up to create a "homogeneous" European land block which would possibly require the removal of Africans from tribal holdings. Finally, the Member revealed that the government was giving serious consideration to the renewal of ninety-nine year leases and to the abolition of the Land Acquisitions Ordinance, which stipulated that Native Authorities had to be consulted before lands could be alienated. Although these announcements proved unfounded and the official involved was subsequently removed from his post, in the interim his statement produced a popular uproar within Great Britain led by the Fabian Bureau.[32]

This period also saw the initiation of a rift between the liberal and conservative factions concerning the supervisory role of the United Nations in the administration of the territory. Liberal interests in the international body's activities dated back to the drawing up of the Trusteeship Agreement. At that time the Fabian Bureau had unsuccessfully utilized its supporters in the House of Commons to attempt to pressure the Secretary of State to consult the indigenous population on their views concerning the nature of the trusteeship contract.[33]

The first truly serious conflict concerning the role of the U.N. came in 1949 with the release of the report of the Visiting Mission. The liberal reform groups as a whole agreed with the criticisms of British policy noted in the document and argued that many of these problems were the product of a vague Colonial Office policy. Rita Hinden commented:

> With the publication of this Report, the fat will be in the fire. Britain critics at UNO will undoubtedly leap with joy at some of the disclosures, and an unmerciful bludgeoning -and probably

at the same time a quite unfair one - may well be
in store for the Colonial Office. British spokesmen will feel their hackles rising and will discant
on all that has already been achieved in the face
of staggering obstacles. Britain has, in fact,
done almost everything she could in a backward,
difficult country with an uneducated population -
everything that is, except have an unambiguous
policy: And it is just this which the irate
Europeans of East Africa are now asking her to
formulate. We want, proclaimed a settlers meeting
in Tanganyika last week, a 'categorical statement
from the Government which will leave nobody, black
or white, in any doubt as to what...the government
intends to do'. Precisely.[34]

The 1945-50 period saw the initiation of yet another
conflict between the liberal and conservative factors of the
home government. This was the question of the rate and
structure of political development within the territory. In
the years to come this one issue was to produce more conflict
within Britain than any other.

During these years, Labour M.P.s repeatedly raised
questions concerning the democratization of native authorities, the initiation and development of democratic processes
in district and provincial councils and administrative plans
for the political education of the indigenous population.
Above all, liberals were interested in the pace at which
elective procedures would be introduced at the territorial
level and in the nature of the alterations to be introduced
in the structure of the territorial government as it under-
went its evolution towards self-rule.[35]

The socialists believed that the Colonial Office and
the territorial administration were willing and able to
initiate a satisfactory plan for political advancement but
that they were being opposed by the overly influential
European community within the trusteeship. White settlers
were therefore viewed as the greatest threat to peaceful
political advancement. The Fabians were convinced that the
tri-racial nature of the territory would present ever
increasing problems to the Crown unless an early declaration
of political development along democratic lines was
announced.[36]

Representative of the socialist position on this matter
was the following policy analysis developed by the Fabians
in 1950:

Tanganyika is at present the storm centre of
a constitutional conflict which has arisen from

22

the proposal that Europeans and non-Europeans should vote on a common electoral roll. This issue is fundamental to the whole future of East and Central Africa.

The problem facing Britain has its roots in the structure of the population of these territories, and we are aware that it is a problem which admits no easy solution...Europeans are overwhelmingly out-numbered by Africans and are also out-numbered by Asiatics, mainly Indians...Considering the great cultural differences between the communities, it is natural that the minority group should feel anxious lest their own cultural standards should be lost, and this would create political difficulties whichever community were in the minority.

It happens, however, that the minority group is at present politically dominant, and that its members, in the light of their own tradition, expect political representation and responsibility of a kind which has been known only in highly advanced communities. If they wish to share democratic institutions with the majority, they face the difficulty that these institutions are very far removed from the traditions of the majority community; if they are unwilling to share power, they can only try to evade or silence African demands for equality.

It appears that in the desire to maintain their own standards intact, the European minorities in the British territories are increasingly turning to the latter policy.[37]

The socialists argued that it was largely in response to white settler pressure that the Crown had developed the policy of racial separation which insured in practice, European dominion of territorial politics. They accordingly viewed the proposed constitutional advances in Tanganyika as "...a test for the whole political future of the territories in East and Central Africa which are inhabited by multi-racial populations."[38]

As the most highly organized and well known of all the liberal activist groups, the Fabian Bureau led the battle within Britain to end racial separation in Tanganyika. The socialists contended that since the ultimate goal of British colonial policy was self-rule through democratic institutions, it was pointless to create artificial barriers which would have to disappear with the emancipation of the territories:

23

...all possible efforts should be directed towards
the development of Parliamentary institutions
which reflect the true balance of interests in
these territories. Separate representation does
not assist in this development, since it institu-
tionalizes the existing division between the
different communities and inhibits the growth of
non-racial political parties. The aim should be
for a common electoral roll for all communities,
with the same qualifications for all electors.[39]

While advocating common roll elections, the socialists
claimed that the quality of the electorate could be safe-
guarded by literacy tests in either Swahili or English,
minimum income requirements and the use of appointed members
for some seats on the Legislative Council.[40] At a meeting
between Fabian Bureau leaders and sympathetic M.P.s, the
liberals devised a temporary plan for African representation
which would allow Tanganyikan blacks who lacked the necessary
economic or educational qualifications to indirectly elect
local representatives to the central legislature through
their native councils. When individual tribal groups were
sufficiently advanced this alternative system could be
phased out.[41] In order to guarantee minority community
representation on the Legislative Council, the Governor
would have the right to nominate members of the Asian and
European races to fill a number of reserved seats. Official
majorities would also be retained on the Legislative and
Executive Councils. Although unofficial appointees would be
selected from all three communities, the liberals insisted
that "...there should be no acceptance in theory or in
practice of any principle of parity of representation or of
any other rigid device."[42] Finally, the liberals agreed
that any political parties which might develop should not be
allowed to limit membership to one race since this would
only further aggravate the racial tensions already produced
by the policy of partnership.

The socialists also rejected the proposals for constitutional development advanced by the Governor in his note to
the Constitutional Committee. They especially resented the
fact that the suggested electoral college system provided a
common electoral roll for the minority groups but excluded
educated Africans. In addition, there was no insurance that
the native authority councils, the supposed training ground
for political participation, would be forced to operate in a
democratic manner.[43]

During this period, in addition to challenging Colonial Office policies, liberal activists regularly offered advice and support to Tanganyikan African leaders. Chief Kidaha Makwaia, one of the four African members of the Legislative Council and an active member of the Fabian Bureau was advised not to support any constitutional changes based on regionalism since this would ultimately lead to sectional feuding and would fail to provide the African elite with the territorial base of political support needed to create a viable national leadership. At the same time, Makwaia was discouraged from accepting any proposal for the reservation of a set percentage of Legislative Council seats for each race since such a settlement would only encourage political competition along racial lines.[44]

The Fabians offered similar advice to Legislative Council appointee and T.A.A. leader Thomas Marealle and to various other members of the Association. In this early period, the T.A.A., although actively involved in local issues, had not yet formulated a definite plan for territorial political evolution. The socialists continually urged the Association to develop such a policy statement. The liberals advised that only a program ultimately based on open elections through a non-racial franchise could guarantee the evolution of truly democratic institutions within the territory. For this reason parity should not be supported. The right of the minority groups to maintain a significant role within the government could be preserved temporarily by minimal franchise qualifications and by the appointive power of the Governor. However, the Bureau urged the Association to make it clear that the territory must eventually have a black-dominated government.[45]

It should be noted that in this period liberals were much more forceful in their protests and had much clearer plans for future territorial development than did the fledgling African activist groups. At the same time, the Fabians were willing to give credence to the Colonial Office's commitment to the eventual creation of a black controlled government in Tanganyika. Their conflict with the home government therefore focused upon the questions of the pace of political evolution towards self-rule and the structure of the political system being evolved in the trusteeship. At no time, however, did the socialists support the claims made by the anti-colonial faction at the United Nations that Britain in fact had no intention of emancipating the territory.

Accordingly, by 1950, the Fabian Colonial Bureau had assumed a demanding and actively aggressive posture on Tanganyika. Socialists were dissatisfied with both the slow moving policies of the Crown and with the rather nebulous and weak demands made by the T.A.A. At the same time, however, they were not blindly committed to a sudden and unplanned rush towards independence as advocated by the more radical members of the Trusteeship Council. Clearly, the Bureau stood as a progressive yet balanced force in the midst of the multiple and conflicting factions concerned with the future of the territory.

CHAPTER III

THE CREATION OF THE SOCIALIST-NATIONALIST ALLIANCE: 1951-1954

Territorial Developments

By 1950 the stage was set for a political controversy of major proportions in Tanganyika. The plans devised by the British government involving the rate and structure of future constitutional development were being challenged by liberal groups within the home government, by the anti-colonial faction at the United Nations and by a number of fledgling African nationalist organizations. These forces stood in clear opposition to the slower pace of political evolution envisioned by the Colonial Office and supported by both the Tory party in Britain and the white settler community within the trusteeship. From 1951 to 1954, new sources of controversy were to increase the tension among these opposing groups and to lead to the formation of a close cooperative alliance between the Fabian socialists and the African nationalists.

Several new administrative decisions contributed to the spread of popular unrest during the period 1951-1954. Key among these was the activation of the Meru land scheme. Although the tribe had petitioned both the 1951 Visiting Mission and the Colonial Office to delay implementation of the plan, the territorial administration decided to begin evacuation of the corridor before the U.N. was able to investigate the matter.

As the number of protests against official policies escalated during these years the Tanganyika government took the first clear steps aimed at restricting African political activity. In August, 1953, the Governor announced that no members of the administrative service of any race could belong to a political association. The ruling was a major blow to the T.A.A. Throughout the territory branch officers reported the loss of their principal leaders.

Undoubtedly, the most suppressive government measure against political activity during this period was the passage of the Registration of Societies Ordinance in 1954. This regulation required all political organizations within the territory to receive government recognition. Any group refused registration was automatically banned from political activity. In addition, registration could be cancelled at any time for societies which "threatened" to disrupt law and order or the peaceful development of the territory.[46]

One major positive step towards constitutional development was that initiated by the colonial government in

January, 1952, when a committee was formed to study the question of a franchise for the territory's first electoral experience. Headed by Prof. W. M. M. Mackenzie, the Special Commission was charged with the task of recommending a program of political development which would ultimately result in the achievement of responsible government with an unofficial majority.[47]

After nine months of research the Mackenzie Commission issued its findings. It suggested the division of the territory into nine constituencies. In the provinces, elections would be based on a common roll from which one member of each race would be elected to represent the province in the Legislative Council. The Commission also recommended that an official majority be preserved in that body. The Mackenzie team suggested that common roll elections be initiated for the European and Asian communities but that African representatives be selected through indirect means or by nomination.

On June 25, 1952, while the Mackenzie Commission was still conducting its investigation, the Secretary of State announced that the United Kingdom had decided to introduce two changes in the political structure of Tanganyika. The first alteration divided the number of seats on the unofficial side of the Legislative Council equally among the three races. The second established parity among the unofficial members of the Executive Council. Significantly, while announcing these changes, the Crown took the opportunity to reaffirm its commitment to indirect rule and its opposition to any timetable for future political development.

Territorial Political Activities: 1951-54

During the 1951-54 period the white settler community of Tanganyika revealed itself as the most reactionary group within the territory. It was adamantly opposed not only to the demands for rapid political advancement made by Tanganyikan Africa nationalists and their liberal supporters, but also to the few cautious steps to increase African participation taken by the colonial regime. The formation of local government councils and the introduction of parity among the unofficials were fiercely resented by the immigrant community. A common charge leveled by whites was that liberal forces within the home government and the communist bloc on the Trusteeship Council were cooperating to undermine the British Empire.

The principal demands made by the settlers community in this period called for further land alienation and increased

white immigration, both in the name of territorial development. The white community also called for an end to trusteeship and for the direct absorption of Tanganyika into the
Empire.

During the period 1951-54, African Nationalist activity
within the Trusteeship grew increasingly military. In 1951
the Shinyanga branch of the T.A.A. petitioned the Trusteeship
Council for the right to elect an African to attend Council
meetings for the purpose of representing indigenous interests. At the same time, the Mwanza branch presented a
petition in which it demanded increased African representation on the Legislative Council, non-racial elections for
all representative bodies within the Trusteeship, and the
opening of high level civil service positions to blacks.[48]

When a Visiting Mission team arrived in Tanganyika in
1954, it discovered that African demands had become much
more radical in the interim three years. The T.A.A. was now
calling for the establishment of a time-table for development
toward self-government which had the approval of the black
population. Furthermore, the Association demanded a statement from the Crown affirming that Tanganyika would soon
have an African dominated government. To begin this transformation, it sought the immediate creation of a black
majority in the Legislative Council.[49]

During this period the Mwanza branch of the T.A.A. had
become an especially militant organization. African unrest
in that district centered around dissatisfaction with compulsory destocking procedures and with the cotton cess tax. In
1953 the T.A.A. branch in neighboring Bukoba district also
assumed a much more forceful position in its resistance to
government policies. The unrest there centered upon dissatisfaction with forced agricultural methods and with the
compulsory production of cash crops. Popular resentment was
so strong that in October the provincial commissioner placed
a ban on all public meetings. On November 25, 1953, the
T.A.A. held a massive rally in defiance of this restriction.
Tear gas and a baton charge were used to disperse the crowd.
Although the T.A.A. petitioned the Governor to form a multi-
racial panel to determine the cause of such widespread
unrest, no official response was given to the often repeated
request.

By 1954 African political activists were acutely aware
that the growing spirit of indigenous unrest could readily
be exploited to recruit new members into the ranks of the
nationalist movement. In order for the African elite to
take full advantage of this situation it was first necessary

29

to greatly strengthen the T.A.A. In 1953 the Association acquired the leadership needed to initiate such a transformation when Julius Nyerere assumed the presidency.[50]

By the time Nyerere became President of the T.A.A., he had already formulated definite opinions concerning various aspects of British rule and the steps necessary to change the established system. His early theories, formulated while he was a student at Edinburgh, reflect the strong influence of the Fabian socialists with whom Nyerere was in close contact throughout his period of residence in Great Britain.

In July, 1954, Nyerere met with T.A.A. leaders for a four day constitutional conference. In addition to changing the name of the organization to the Tanganyika African National Union (TANU), membership in the party was now limited to persons of the African race. The new constitution pledged members not to cease militant activities until the territory achieved total independence. In a clear rejection of parity, partnership, and indirect rule, the constitution demanded the immediate holding of open elections for local and territorial offices, the establishment of a black majority on all representative bodies, and the termination of all racial distinctions in the formulation of administrative policy.

The fledgling Union soon found itself in the midst of a major crisis centered around the widespread traditional unrest in the rural areas and especially in Sukumaland. The most significant confrontation occurred in October, 1954, when a series of demonstrations against local chiefs were instigated by TANU militants in the Lake Province. On October 27, the Registrar of Societies announced that the Government would no longer recognize the registration of the Lake Province branch of TANU. Several Union leaders were subsequently deported from the Province and prohibited from participation in political activities elsewhere in the territory.

A similar series of events occurred when the Malampaka branch of TANU engaged in organized protest against the enforcement of official agricultural regulations. In November, the Union district cell there was closed for violation of the Registration of Societies Ordinance. Julius Nyerere began an active campaign to force the Administration to substantiate its charges against the branches involved. The Government, however, refused to prosecute the cases thus leading nationalists to the claim that the Sukuma closings were acts of unjustifiable supression.

The U.N. and the Liberation Drive

In the period 1951-54, two visiting missions toured Tanganyika and produced reports which were highly critical of British administration of the trusteeship.

The Crown's handling of the Meru land case was the cause of especially strong dissatisfaction within the United Nations. The fact that the move had taken place while the Trusteeship Council was still deliberating a petition from the tribe produced a stream of protests from the anti-imperialist members of the international body, who successfully proposed a resolution critical of Britain's handling of the entire episode.[51]

During this period members of the Council also challenged the British policies of racial separation and of parity representation. In March, 1954, its members resolved that the Administering Authority should be required to "intensify efforts to bring about, in the shortest possible time, development of a united Tanganyika, in which the indigenous inhabitants will play their full part."[52]

The 1954 Visiting Mission carefully examined the goals and membership of recently reconstructed TANU. Its official report noted that the Union's leadership was composed of an educated, experienced elite who well articulated the African population's grievances with the administration as well as their aspiration for rapid political development at the territorial level. The report also supported TANU'S objections to the parity system and endorsed its goal of establishing a government based on black majority representation. The most significant statement contained in the Visiting Mission Report was its conclusion that Tanganyika would be ready for independence within a twenty-five year period.

Fabian Bureau Activities: 1951-1954

In 1950 general elections in Britain resulted in the return to power of the Conservative Party. Realizing that the new government would assume a cautious posture towards the political evolution of the dependencies, Secretary Rita Hinden projected that the East and Central African territories would constitute "the major danger point in the Empire."[53] In order to protect the gains they had achieved while in office, the socialists were determined to use their question-time on the floor of Parliament to badger the Conservative regime to introducing rapid political advances in the dependencies.[54] The stage was, therefore, set for further confrontations between the liberal and Tory factions over the evolution of Tanganyika.

31

Of special interest to the socialists were the emerging African political organizations. The Fabian Bureau had never been truly satisfied with the moderate activities and goals of the T.A.A. During the period of the Mathew Commission investigations, the Fabians had complained bitterly that the Association had failed to keep them informed concerning latest developments within the territory. At the same time, they noted that the organization was hesitant to make public its own guidelines for constitutional advancement. Similarly, when the Bureau tried to determine the true facts concerning government opposition to the Chagga Union, an active black association, the T.A.A. was most hesitant about becoming openly involved in the controversy. The socialists were soon led to the conclusion that the fear of job loss kept T.A.A members from assuming a more active role in territorial policies.[55]

It was this lack of cooperation which ultimately led the Fabians to openly criticize the T.A.A. as a "passive" group who were "far too conciliatory" to the colonial regime.[56] The socialists were therefore delighted when Nyerere assumed the presidency of the Association. Because of the close working relationship that had developed between Nyerere and the Fabians during the TANU leader's student days at Edinburgh, the Bureau was confident of his eagerness to cooperate closely with them in their efforts to direct public opinion in the home government in favor of rapid political development within the territory.[57]

During the 1951-54 period the socialists were actively involved with practically all of the sensitive issues which arose in the trusteeship. Especially distasteful to the Fabians was the territorial governments' refusal to allow civil servants to engage in political activities. Since most African elite were employed by the administration, such a policy eliminated much of the potential black leadership from the political arena. While writing to the TANU cell leaders at Mwapachu, Fabian Secretary Nicholson summarized the Bureau's feelings on this issue:

> I don't see why the gap between political activities of other citizens and those permitted civil servants should be so enormous, and particularly why political restrictions should be applied to teachers. I have sent a copy to Mr. Nyerere and hope he will do something about it. As you say, the potential leaders are in the civil service, and if they are all paralyzed it is inevitable that leadership will pass into the hands of possibly less educated people outside.[58]

The Fabians began an active protest campaign in opposition to this policy. M.P.s John Hynd and Frank Beswick both raised the issue repeatedly in the House of Commons and the entire July, 1954, issue of Venture was devoted to an examination of the controversial question.

The socialists were also actively involved in the highly volatile issues of white settlement and land alienation. In February, 1951, Labour M. P. James Johnson demanded that the Secretary of State provide an assurance that whites employed by the faltering Groundnut Scheme would not be permitted to remain in Tanganyika as permanent settlers once the project collapsed.[59] Similarly, in May, 1952, and February, 1954, when rumors concerning increased white settlement and the creation of 99 year leases began to circulate, the Fabian Bureau arranged to have liberal M.P.s raise a series of questions on the floor of Commons.[60] Although both incidents proved to be the products of hearsay and misinterpreted policy statements, the speed and the intensity with which the Bureau addressed the matters is a measure of the socialist commitment to serve as the defender of Tanganyikan interests in the home government.

In June, 1954, when the Colonial administration again raised the possibility of increased European immigration, the Bureau initiated a major campaign to protect Africans from the danger of further white settlement. The socialists demanded seats for Africans on the Immigration Committee and proposed that it be empowered to ensure the adoption of its suggestions.[61] Marjorie Nicholson was assigned the task of visiting the territory for a firsthand analysis of the situation. Based on her interviews with the representatives of the three racial communities, she concluded that no effective government machinery existed to enforce the immigration quotas established by the Colonial Office.[62] Finally, when Chief Makwaia of the Legislative Council visited Britain in June the Bureau interviewed him extensively to gain insights concerning the European settler problem.

When the related issue of land alienation was raised by a Meru Citizens Union's petition to the U.N. the Fabian Bureau quickly brought the question to the floor of the Commons to determine exactly what had occurred during the controversial move. However, once it became clear that the transfer had indeed been necessary and did not constitute part of an overall plan to create a zone of segregated white settlement, the Fabians issued a clear statement of support for the scheme.[63] Accordingly, the Bureau revealed that its disagreements with the Colonial Office were based on concrete

33

issues and were not merely ideological attacks against the symbols of the colonial order. Frequent examples of such moderation were to be found throughout the 1945-1961 period.

The socialists also began an active campaign to try to force the Colonial Office to insure that Africans in Tanganyika were made aware of the activities of the Trustee-ship Council. Coupled with this was a demand that the indigenous population be advised of their rights to petition the United Nations without the approval of either the terri-torial administration or the Colonial Office.[64]

The Fabians also strongly supported African demands for rapid political advancement. When the Labour regime was removed from office via the 1950 elections, the socialists immediately began to formulate plans for a campaign to issue that despite this setback, a dramatic increase in African political participation in all of the East African territor-ies did occur. In 1951 Selwyn-Clarke confided to J. H. Lodge, M.P., that the Bureau feared that in "the case of Tanganyika, the change of Government may have set the clock back," and that accordingly extensive plans were being devised to help advance the cause of political evolution in the trusteeship.[65] Outgoing Secretary of State Creech-Jones initiated a campaign aimed at making the British public aware of the reforms needed if peaceful development were to be preserved in the territory. His writings and public statements called for a pace of political evolution which would match the rapid advances being made in the fields of economics and education through the Colonial Development programs. At the same time he stressed the failure of the[66] tri-racial system and the inadequacies of indirect rule.

While the socialists were in favor of the rapid initia-tion of majority rule, they were by no means insensitive to the plight of the European community. Although opposed to partnership as an imbalanced form of representation, they also rejected any African proposals aimed at depriving Europeans of a voice in the independent government. Speaking of this concern, Creech-Jones noted:

> If 'partnership' arouses African fears, 'democracy' must arouse European fears. 'One man, one vote, and a Gold Coast constitution' have become the symbols of a fear that a small white community will ultimately be engulfed by a black flood. Some African spokesmen have confirmed their fears by talking of an 'African Nation' in which Europeans will remain as 'guests'. While we hold the view that immigrant communities should

not be permanently privileged, we believe equally that immigrants who are already settled in East and Central Africa and who owe their first loyalty to the Crown and to the country in which they now live and bring up their children must be accepted by Africans as part of the local population, and that all should have their share in building a democratic society based on the equality of individuals. This conception requires that Africans as well as the immigrants should be prepared for the compromises which democracy demands from all individuals and without which it cannot exist.[67]

In order to avoid racial oppression from any source, the Fabians advocated the initiation of a qualified open franchise on a non-racial basis in Tanganyika. While realizing that African lack of training and experience made universal adult suffrage immediately impractical, they insisted that the use of high voting qualifications and the reservation of seats for specific communities were acceptable only as temporary measures. The Fabians consistently maintained that political participation as well as economic and social development had to be along non-racial lines. Rather than stress the factors which separated the three communities they believed that the goal of British policy should be the elimination of ethnic distinctions.[68]

When the Mackenzie Report was released, Labour M.P.s, encouraged and assisted by the Fabian Bureau, utilized their speaking time in the House of Commons to demand that its suggestions concerning non-racial elections for Dar es Salaam as well as the election of unofficial members for the rest of the territory be initiated immediately. The Tory regime however, refused to concede to liberal demands for a timetable of political advancement. Noting the storm of controversy raised by the Labour M.P.s and the Fabian Bureau, the T.A.A. General Secretary wrote:

> It is very gratifying to see how prompt our allies in Britain have been in pressing for a discussion of the recommendations in the House of Commons. We here appreciate and well realize the value of your support.[69]

The year 1954 found the rival factions within the home government divided on a number of other issues concerning the political evolution of Tanganyika. In the spring of that year Nyerere began to press for a reconstruction of the Legislative Council based on the guidelines of the Mackenzie report. Specifically, he sought the introduction of common roll elections with reserved seats for the municipality of Dar es Salaam. However, when Labour M. P. James Johnson was persuaded by the Fabian Bureau to raise the issue in the House of Commons, Secretary of State Lyttleton made it clear that the Tory government would not consider the proposal. Battle lines between the Tory and Labour parties were quickly drawn over the question of territorial political advancement. The Bureau made it clear that it intended to support the nationalists in their demand for the incorporation of the Mackenzie report recommendations. In reporting to TANU on the adamant position taken by the Secretary of State against the reconstruction of the legislative body, Fabian Secretary Nicholson commented:

This position still remains most unsatisfactory to us, and I presume that Mr. Nyerere will be raising the issue in the Legislative Council. We shall continue to do what we can at this end.[70]

During the period of political unrest which culminated with the banning of TANU in Sukumaland, the socialists rallied to the support of the African nationalists. When the Lake Province confrontations began, T.A.A. leaders maintained a constant stream of correspondence with both the Fabian Bureau and the Labour Party. The liberals, in turn, pressed Parliament for a full-scale investigation of the situation and demanded the immediate reopening of all party branches if the government could not produce indictments which listed specific offenses and named the individuals involved. In April 1954, Labour Leader Fenner Brockway demanded that the Secretary of State explain why Governor Twining had refused to meet with a T.A.A. delegation upon his recent visit to Mwanza. At the same time he challenged the use of tear gas to disperse the Bukoba branch rally of December 2, 1953. The Secretary refused to respond to these issues.

In July, 1954, protests against native authorities coupled with resentment over an increase in the cattle tax produced widespread unrest in the Mwanza region. Brockway raised the issue in Parliament, warning that government policy was causing unnecessary tension. This in turn produced Conservative accusations that the Labour Party was undermining the Crown's plans for territorial development.[71] Speaking of the cooperation the nationalists were receiving from the liberals in Britain and especially from the Fabians, Mwanza T.A.A. leader Munanka stated:

Again we have been filled with joy to read about our distinguished fighter Mr. Brockway on the question of Cattle and Cotton Cess and Stock limitation. We immediately informed our people about it. Although the answers from the Secretary of States [sic] were not fully satisfying, but we have been left assured that something good might emerge from it. We sent full information to our Honourable Friend to pursue the matter further as our people are still not happy on this question. We wish him to continue until such time that we hear the Government stop Livestock Limitation Policies.[72]

In August the Fabian Bureau dispatched Marjorie Nicholson to Tanganyika to personally examine the situation in the Lake Province. Her subsequent report encouraged liberals to continue their criticism of the native authority system and their attack on the slow pace of political development. In summarizing her findings, Nicholson concluded:

> I am very worried about the undercurrents in Tanganyika. The Government gets away with looking very liberal as it is when compared with its neighbors, but I think there is far too much complacency about. A little prodding from this end might be helpful.[73]

When the TANU branches in Sukumaland were finally closed a lively correspondence ensued between militant black activists and James Betts of the Fabian Bureau. Working in close cooperation, the Africans supplied the socialists with information concerning the latest developments in the troubled region. The Bureau in turn utilized this information to repeatedly raise issues in Parliament. On December 8, M. P. John Hynd initiated a debate on the subject in the House of Commons. Based on the fact that the outbreaks had been isolated and the possibility that the parties involved had not been properly informed of the nature of their offenses, he suggested that the banned TANU branches be reopened. This suggestion was rejected by the Secretary of State.

Thus, by 1954, the home government was markedly divided over the question of political developments within the trusteeship. The liberal faction, encouraged by the appearance of capable African leadership and the creation of a territorial-wide political organization, sought rapid political advancement along non-racial lines. It was clear that a close alliance was being formed between the Fabians and the African Nationalists. However, the socialists remained objective in their analysis and refused to support the

extremist demands and accusations emanating either from the
black leadership or from the anti-colonial faction on the
Trusteeship Council.

CHAPTER IV

THE DEBATE OVER CONSTITUTIONAL DEVELOPMENT: 1955-1957

Background

During the period 1955-57 the Colonial Office began to introduce plans to outline the future course of political development in Tanganyika. The alterations proposed by the British were clearly designed to offer the promise of gradual and peaceful change and, at the same time, to keep intact the principles of parity, indirect rule, and partnership.

In March, 1955, a new Legislative Council was convened, based on parity of unofficial members as recommended in the Mathew Report. In addition, the Executive Council now contained six unofficials (two from each race).

One month later, Governor Twining announced that he intended to introduce a limited, highly qualitative franchise in the territory. Substantial economic and educational qualifications were required which eliminated the bulk of the African population from both the franchise and candidacy. A ban on civil servant participation and mandatory fees for candidates also resulted in the exclusion of many educated Africans.

On May 26, the Governor established a committee to review his proposals for franchise requirements. The nine man panel was composed of five Europeans, two Africans, and two Asians. Six of its members were unofficials on the Legislative Council and were also members of a newly founded white settler political association, the United Tanganyika Party (UTP). When the committee released its findings in October the qualifications it proposed were exactly the same as those articulated by the Governor.

Finally, in April, 1957, Twining announced that a Post Elections Committee would be appointed to examine the results of the first territorial elections for Legislative Council seats which were scheduled for late 1958 in a select number of constituencies. The committee would evaluate the results of this contest and then make recommendations concerning the methods, procedures, and date for the holding of elections in the remaining constituencies of the trusteeship.

During this period it became increasingly apparent that the native authorities were losing control over large segments of the indigenous population. There was a marked increase in popular dissatisfaction with local administrators, taxes, and official agricultural policies. In order to curb widespread unrest, in November, 1955, the Legislative

Council approved the Incitement to Violence Act which made the passing of oral remarks critical of another race a crime of sedition. In the trying of such cases the burden of proof was placed on the defendant.

Coupled with this legislation was the even more stringent Penal Code Amendment Bill. This law, as revised, gave the government especially wide latitude in the prosecution of dissidents and empowered the Governor to ban the past and future works of any author considered dangerous.

Finally, the administration made clear its belief that local TANU leaders were the initiators of many of the incidents of civil disobedience. In April, 1957, the Tanganyika Public Relations Department released a pamphlet entitled "What's the Answer?", in which it openly accused TANU of inciting the indigenous population to commit unlawful acts and of encouraging them to ignore the traditional sources of authority. The publication strongly discouraged Africans from joining TANU and ended with an appeal for indigenous cooperation with the native administrators.

Political Activities Within The Territory

As the conflict between TANU and the government escalated in the 1955-57 period, the minority communities took steps to effectively articulate their views concerning the course of political development.

In February, 1956, the first truly viable white settler organization appeared in the form of the United Tanganyika Party (UTP) which was unquestionably an indirect agency of the colonial administration. The party was created on February 24, during a meeting between the unofficial members of the Legislative Council and Governor Twining, in the home of the latter.[74] In an attempt to create a political organization to oppose the radical goals of TANU, the UTP drew up a Manifesto in which it advocated multi-racialism, the maintenance of parity, and political evolution guided by traditional authorities.

Although it had only a small base of support, the UTP presented a serious threat to TANU. The party claimed the loyalty of 28 of the 30 unofficial members of the Legislative Council. As such, it dominated the committee created by the Government to consider the questions of both elections and franchise for 1958.

It was during this period that the Asian Association became actively interested in territorial politics for the first time. Under the leadership of its President Amir H. Jamal, the Association tried to persuade Asians to abandon

40

their isolationist tendencies and to become involved in the pressing political issues of the period.

While most Asians did not respond to the Association's plea for increased political participation, those who did constituted the more liberal elements of the community and showed great sympathy for the TANU cause. Many Association organizers, including Jamal himself, were also active members of the Fabian Society. Accordingly, they cooperated with both TANU and the socialists to promote the goal of self-government.[75]

In the period 1955-57, the Tanganyika African National Union transformed itself from a struggling association into a well-coordinated political party which became the organizational embodiment of the nationalist movement. This change was due in a large measure to the decision made by Nyerere to devote all of his time to the expansion of TANU and to the close support the Union enjoyed from the liberal elements in the home government. In March, 1955, the TANU president resigned from his teaching position. For several months Nyerere avoided public appearances and corresponded continuously with liberal supporters in Britain and especially with his contacts within the Fabian Bureau. By September, he had, with their help formulated the future political objectives of TANU.

One of Nyerere's major goals was to evolve a territorial base of popular support for the Union. His efforts were greatly aided by the April, 1955, publication of the recent Visiting Mission report, which identified his party as the one organization within the territory capable of leading an independence movement. A sudden influx of new members for TANU followed the release of the document and consisted primarily of recruits from the westernized elements of the African population.

At the same time, membership from the traditional sector also swelled. In 1955, Nyerere's chief lieutenant, Oscar Kambona, began a three month tour of the territory designed to bring the TANU message to the more isolated areas. He soon discovered that dissatisfaction with both agricultural policies and with the native authorities was so widespread that non-westernized Tanganyikan Africans were eager to join the party.

In this period the government made several attempts to persuade TANU to pursue a course of political development which would be within, rather than outside of, official channels. As part of this effort, on August 2, 1957, Governor Twining unexpectedly announced the appointment of Nyerere to the Legislative Council.

41

Nyerere attended only two meetings of the Council, during which he submitted proposals calling for the end of parity and indirect rule. All of Nyerere's demands, however, were either ignored by the government or defeated in debate by the Council's UTP faction. As a result the TANU president resigned his seat, protesting that the administration did not understand the art of compromise and that the UTP in effect controlled the Legislative Council. In a letter to the Fabian Bureau, Nyerere stated that the government was trying to "pacify TANU through bribery" and that continued service on the Legislative Council would "amount to hypocrisy".[76]

By October, 1956, TANU leaders were convinced that the administration had no intention of altering the systems of parity and indirect rule. They therefore drew up and widely circulated their own proposals for constitutional development. Foremost among TANU demands was the Union's insistence that the Government recognize that Tanganyika would evolve into a "primarily African State."[77] In order to advance toward this goal, the Union demanded the introduction of ministerial posts in the Executive Council with portfolios for both official and representative members. In addition, TANU insisted that half of the seats be reserved for Africans.

The party's most radical demands were contained in its goals for the transformation of the Legislative Council. The Union accepted the preservation of an official majority on the government side of the floor but insisted that parity between Africans and non-Africans be introduced there. Nationalist demands for the unofficial side were far more dramatic. TANU called for the abolition of the triple vote and for the introduction of a modified version of parity based on equality between African and non-African representatives. It also demanded the initiation of universal adult suffrage.

Between 1954 and 1957 Nyerere made three separate trips to the United Nations to present TANU demands to the Trusteeship Council. His 1956 itinerary included two separate visits to United Nations headquarters as well as extensive meetings with Labour Party leaders and with representatives of the Fabian Society in Great Britain.

It gradually became apparent that the administration and TANU were on the verge of a major confrontation. The first incident to indicate an escalation of hostilities occurred in February, 1957, when the administration placed a six month ban on Nyerere which prohibited him from addressing public meetings. The Government claimed that the TANU president had been stirring up racial animosity and that he had publicly advocated resistance to both local administrators and official policies.

Nyerere denied that his speeches had in any way encouraged his audience to violate the law. He demanded that the government produce evidence of his misdeeds and insisted that he was being persecuted by administrative officials who sought to undermine TANU's good reputation. The administration, however, refused to reply to the challenge. Nyerere then sought the aid of the Fabians who readily agreed to raise the issue in the House of Commons.[78]

In the period 1955-57, serious confrontations continued to occur in the more isolated sectors of the territory between TANU cells and local colonial administrators. The closing of isolated TANU cells was a common tactic employed by the government in its battle with the Union during this period. Virtually all were closed for minor acts of insubordination to local authorities.

The United Nations: International Criticism of British Policy

During the period 1955-57, the Trusteeship Council once again became the site of an ideological conflict. The first major confrontation occurred in February, 1955, during the debate over the recently released 1954 Visiting Mission Report. The United Kingdom representative condemned the document as "impractical" and "shortsighted", because of its recommendation for a twenty-five year target date for independence. The anti-colonial forces, by contrast, strongly supported the deadline.

During the debate of the 1954 report it became clear that ideological commitments sharply divided the Council on virtually every issue concerning Tanganyika. Britain's repeated attempts to explain the factual dimensions surrounding any of her policy decisions were routinely condemned by her critics on the Council as needed efforts to justify the maintenance of minority rule and the preservation of her empire.

In their final evaluation of the Visiting Mission findings, the Council members concluded that although the Administering Authority had attempted to foster racial cooperation it was, nonetheless, necessary to immediately grant Africans more participation in all levels of government. It stressed the necessity of fostering a sense of "territorial consciousness" and recommended the eventual establishment of a common roll vote.[79]

The following year the Trusteeship Council again considered the question of political development in Tanganyika as a result of persistent urging from the U.S.S.R. When pressed to define the United Kingdom's position on the pace of political evolution, the British representation announced that:

> It is unthinkable that those responsible for carrying on Her Majesty's Government could, in the discharge of their duties under the Trusteeship System, plot out a timed course of political development for a Trust territory based on nothing more than guesswork.[80]

Nonetheless, on April 9, 1956, the Council adopted a recommendation to establish a series of target dates for political, economic, and educational development, designed "to bring the British-administered U.N. trust territory of Tanganyika to the final goal of self-government or independence."[81]

Another major controversy arose in 1957 following the publication of the report of that year's Visiting Mission. During its tour, the team conducted over a dozen interviews with TANU leaders and in particular with members of the Executive Committee of the Union. The Mission concluded that TANU had formulated a viable plan for the establishment of a moderate, African-controlled state in which the immigrant communities would enjoy equal rights as citizens.

The report suggested that major changes be made in the territory's existing administrative policy to make provision for increased African political awareness. Specifically, they contended that the system of parties would have to be terminated and that the non-African communities would have to abandon their monopoly over territorial resources. The Mission also called upon the administration to introduce universal adult franchise.

The Fabian Bureau: A Balanced Support for Nationalism

During the 1954-57 period, the liberal and conservative forces within the home government assumed opposing positions on most of the controversial issues concerning the trusteeship. The attitude of the socialists was clearly expressed by Fabian Bureau Chief Marjorie Nicholson in her report following a two month visit to the trusteeship in 1955:

> There are very serious undercurrents at work in Tanganyika although the Tanganyika Government presently is presenting to the world a picture of a very happy country...the tone of the Government

comments, and particularly the tone of its references to politically conscious Africans, is quite
out of tune with the progressive policy the Government claims to be following...

Members of the Parliament have raised a
number of questions following my visit...and in
all cases but one have received negative answers,
some complacent, some frivolous. There is a blind
spot on the whole question of political advance
and political education.[82]

The most controversial political issue dividing the two
factions in the home government centered around the colonial
administration's attitude toward TANU. Liberals claimed
that the territorial government was adamantly opposed to the
Union and consequently that it deliberately persecuted the
nationalists. The multiple restrictions placed on the
organization were accordingly viewed not as steps necessary
to preserve law and order but rather as attempts to thwart
the growth of the independence movement.

The Fabians continually stressed that TANU and, in
particular, Nyerere offered a moderate and gradual solution
to many of the potentially flammable issues within the
territory. They argued that unless some recognition and
concessions were granted to the Union, the more radical and
violent elements of the African population would rise to
power. At no time, however, did the liberals challenge the
good intentions or ultimate goals of Colonial Office plans.
In a letter to the Secretary of State, Fabian Secretary
Selwyn-Clarke conceded:

My committee does not wish to exaggerate the
seriousness of current trends in Tanganyika. It
is aware that the administration is generally
acceptable to the people, that it is pursuing a
sound policy of economic and social advancement,
and that in the political field it is working on
lines intended to alleviate racial antagonism.[83]

However, the Bureau insisted that despite its good
intentions, the British policy "did not all take into account
the rapid spread of the nationalist spirit" and that the
Colonial Office was discouraged from making substantial
alterations in its methods as a result of pressure from the
minority communities within the territory.

The socialists argued that if Nyerere were to receive
more cooperation from the government the danger of racial
violence could be avoided:

The President of TANU is a very able young
man, quiet in his methods, moderate in his opinions

45

and generally anxious that racial antagonism should be avoided.

...We feel that the comments concerning Nyerere in the observations are entirely at variance with our impressions and bear a striking resemblance to earlier comments on other African politicians who are now Ministers in other territories.[84]

The Labour Party agreed with the Fabian Bureau's analysis and warned that within the trusteeship:

...a racialist spirit is beginning to creep into African organizations and this racial tension will probably increase unless Government shows some willingness to recognize the moderate TANU organization.[85]

The close bonds which had long united TANU and the Fabian socialists grew even stronger during the period 1954-57. Correspondence between Bureau and TANU leaders by this time was virtually all on a first name basis. Nyerere himself strongly encouraged socialist support and repeatedly made it clear that "the spread of TANU's message in Britain by our liberal allies is essential to the achievement of our goals.[86]

During the period when the Union was formulating its official demands for franchise requirements and Legislative Council restructuring the Labour Party and the Fabian Bureau maintained especially close contacts with the TANU hierarchy. Prior to each of Nyerere's appearance before the United Nations, the Union leader visited London and held private meetings with friendly M.P.'s who offered tactical advice concerning the problem of political advancement. Often TANU leaders would reside in the homes of prominent socialists during their visits.[87]

In December, 1955, TANU established a permanent personal contact within the home government when Oscar Kambona took up residence in London to complete his study of law. While in Britain he served in an almost daily capacity as a liaison between the Union and its supporters. TANU would frequently instruct Kambona to deliver personal messages to cooperative M.P.'s or to address liberal groups to explain Union policy. The reformers, in turn, deluged Kambona with questions concerning TANU's goals, situations within the trusteeship and the personal motivations of numerous members of both the Union and the colonial administration.[88] So close was the spirit of cooperation between the socialists and nationalists during these years official policy statements issued by the Labour Party were often formulated with the consultation of TANU representatives.

46

The Fabians, by the same token, enjoyed great influence with TANU. When the date for the first territorial elections was announced, D. F. Heath, a liberal white settler and member of the Fabian Society sought the Bureau's help in receiving an endorsement from Nyerere to run for the European seat in the Dar es Salaam constituency. Heath realized that TANU approval was necessary for any non-African candidate who hoped to capture a majority of the African votes under the tri-racial ballot system. Seeking the aid of James Betts, a long time friend of both Heath and Nyerere, the white farmer stated:

> I wrote to Nyerere after his return from U.K., which must have been nearly a month ago, but have had no reply so far. I have also called on Rattansey, who is now vice-president of the Asian Society; and we had a long political chat. I think I am pretty certain of sufficient Asian support, but am still a bit doubtful of TANU, as it is difficult, but understandable, for an Englishman, no matter how sincere are his motives, to get an entry into the xenophobic and esoteric circle of educated Africans. As I told you, I know Nyerere slightly and have given him lunch, but he may well believe that that was just idle curiosity. I think a letter from you --from a source he trusts -- would be a very great help to me...[89]

When Betts subsequently endorsed Heath in a letter to Nyerere, the TANU president agreed to support the white settler's candidacy and he was subsequently elected.

During this period of close cooperation three liberal TANU supporters, Marjorie Nicholson of the Fabian Bureau, Arthur Skeffington, M.P., and John Hatch, M.P., visited the trusteeship to gain first-hand information concerning political developments. Kambona reported that the visit of John Hatch, who was the Labour Party Commonwealth Officer, was a strong encouragement to Africans and that Hatch's public endorsement of TANU greatly aided the Union's recruitment drive during this critical period.[90] The Fabian Bureau performed an additional service to the Union by maintaining close correspondence with many of the more moderate to liberal members of the minority communities. The socialists repeatedly urged progressive Asians and Europeans to co-operate with TANU for the well-being of all of the residents of the trusteeship.[91]

47

Finally, throughout the 1954-57 period of tense negotiations, sympathetic members of Parliament raised repeated questions on the floor of Commons to challenge Tory policies and to advocate the course of territorial evolution suggested by the nationalists. The liberal allies of TANU used their positions as members of Parliament to attack virtually all of the government plans which the nationalist movement found objectionable. They were especially critical of the measures taken by the Tanganyikan government to curtail the activities of African political agitators. In March, 1955, M.P. John Hynd demanded an explanation of the Registration of Societies Ordinance, which he viewed as an oppressive and unnecessary measure. The Secretary of State defended the legislation by pointing out that it had been widely praised by several non-official members of the Legislative Council and by several native authorities. Liberals, however, refused to accept this reasoning and insisted that chiefs who stood to gain by the undermining of the nationalist drive, were not reliable sources of information concerning indigenous attitudes.[92]

As a result of repeated requests from TANU, the liberals agreed to pursue the matter within the House of Commons. Speaking of their dissatisfaction with the Colonial Office position on the ordinance, Fabian Secretary Nicholson remarked to Nyerere that "...the Ordinance seems to me quite abominable and should also be unnecessary if everything in Tanganyika is as rosy as the Government always claims.[93]

The Fabian Bureau, despite its ideological commitment to the Union's goals, nonetheless continued to maintain its reasonable and balanced approach in its evaluation of territorial affairs. When TANU appealed to the socialists for aid in opposing the ban on civil servant participation in political organizations, the Bureau assigned several staff members the task of investigating the issue. When research revealed that such restrictions were generally in force throughout the Empire, the Bureau concluded that TANU could not justly oppose the ban, despite Nyerere's contention that it would isolate his Union from large elements of the capable African leadership.[94]

The liberals were by contrast severely critical of the Penal Code (Amendment) Ordinance, which they condemned in the Commons as a deviation from the model British Penal Code, by placing the burden of proof on the accused. When John Hynd failed to receive a satisfactory justification for the measure while in debate, the Fabian Bureau urged him to press the Secretary of State for an explanation.[95] Shortly thereafter, Oscar Kambona was called upon to explain TANU's viewpoint on this issue. The nationalist leader reported that the Governor had refused to discuss the Ordinance with a Union deputation before it was enacted. He also complained that since its passage "...it is almost impossible to make any political statement that doesn't cause dissatisfaction to the members of other communities."[96] The issue was again raised by M.P.s White and Hynd on February 22. The liberals demanded a detailed explanation from the Lenox-Boyd, clarifying why this unique piece of legislation had been designed for Tanganyika and for no other dependency.[97] The aggressive action of the liberals was motivated by their belief that the ordinance was designed solely as an impediment to TANU and that "conditions in Tanganyika provide no justification whatsoever for such legislation."[98] The Secretary of State, however, refused to give a detailed response. He stated that no particular incident had inspired the legislation, but rather, that it was the produce of "the general desirability of discouraging such acts."[99] Although the issue was raised again by Labour M.P.s on February 28 and March 1, Lennox-Boyd refused to further elaborate on the matter.

By far the most controversial questions separating the liberal and conservative factions were their views on the parity system and the closely related issue of territorial elections. The Tory party persistently argued that parity had to be maintained until the economic and educational gap separating the African and non-African communities was substantially narrowed. At the same time, they felt that the election proposals devised by the Tanganyikan government were more than generous and that any attempt to further accelerate the pace of political evolution would lead to disaster. The liberals, by contrast, insisted that parity must be replaced by a program of rapid political development in order to obviate the danger of racial violence emanating from the increasingly restless majority community.

The liberals contended that the moderate philosophy of TANU had prevented any serious outbreaks of racial unrest up to that date but that unless the administration set a deadline for the termination of parity, more radical elements might well gain control of the independence drive. This argument was summarized by Selwyn-Clarke in an open letter to the Secretary of State:

> Racial parity has been accepted by the present
> African leaders, but they definitely regard it as
> a state which will not last for a considerable
> period. My Committee suggests that it should be

49

clearly stated immediately that the policy of the
United Kingdom and the Tanganyika Government is
that Tanganyika shall ultimately be a self-
governing democratic state. In the absence of
such a statement, Tanganyika is drawn into the
discussion of what is meant by such terms as
'partnership' and multi-racial state', and many
Africans have formed the impression that parity is
a fraud, designed to prevent them from ever having
control of their own country. Demands for an
'African' state are already heard and racism is
already raising its head.[100]

On June 28, 1956, the Working Committee of the Fabian
Bureau met to discuss the problem of parity. The socialists
formulated a policy statement which demanded that the Crown
publicly recognize that "the ultimate aim of all multi-racial
societies is a common electoral roll with universal adult
suffrage", and that if the temporary use of parity were
absolutely necessary "it must be done on a basis of equal
requirements for the franchise."[101] In October, the Labour
Party Annual Conference at Blackpool produced a political
pamphlet entitled The Plural Society outlining its official
colonial policy. At that time, the delegates passed the
following resolution concerning parity:

Firstly, the people in the colonies with mixed
racial societies must ultimately have the right to
decide under which type of constitution they wish
to live. The Westminister model is not necessarily
the best for all societies of mixed races, and
secondly, the best way to give them the opportunity
to make their decision is through the election of
representatives by universal adult suffrage on the
basis of one man one vote...
...the hope of survival of the minorities, on a
long-term basis, lies in the ability of Africans,
Indians, and Europeans to exclude race and colour
and the prejudices and resentments they arouse and
to think of themselves as citizens of Kenya,
Tanganyika or Northern Rhodesia.[102]

Several weeks later former Secretary of State James
Griffiths, who at that time was serving as chief spokesman
for the Labour Party on colonial affairs, issued a policy
statement in which he criticized parity as an impractical
and outdated policy which produced unnecessary racial
tensions. Griffiths argued that peaceful cooperation along

non-racial lines was the only real solution to the problems
facing the plural societies:

> ...the rights of the Indian and European minorities
> will be secured by the leadership and service that
> they can give to the territory...
>
> No member of the Labour Party should under-
> estimate the long struggle ahead to achieve the
> policy approved by our annual conference.
>
> When we agree on these policies we must mean
> it; when a Labour Government comes to power it
> means that if these people get it we must do
> without it. If we are not prepared to go without,
> do not let us pass resolutions that mean nothing.
> But we mean it, so let us be ready to stand up and
> meet the critics who say, "We should get this, not
> the blacks."[103]

In order to insure that the liberal view on parity
always had a spokesman, Fabian Bureau Director Eirene White
was assigned the task of representing the Labour Party in
any Parliamentary debate which might arise over the question
of race relations in Tanganyika.[104]   Clearly then, both the
Labour Party and the Fabian Bureau were closely aligned to
TANU in their views concerning parity and the needs of
Africans living in the plural societies.

The liberals also maintained that unless a system of
franchise qualifications were devised which gave the vote to
a majority of adult Africans, the moderate position of the
nationalist drive in Tanganyika would soon be replaced by a[105]
far more radical and violent form of protest.   Accordingly, in April, 1955, the Bureau demanded that the Secretary
of State create a special committee on Tanganyika, comprised
of representatives of all races, to consider the question of
franchise qualifications for both local and central government elections.[106]   During that year socialist M.P.s con-
fronted Lennox-Boyd on no fewer than thirty occasions with
demands that the indigenous population of Tanganyika be
educated in modern electoral procedures to prepare them for[107]
participation in the coming political contests.

The liberal activists, however, refrained from detailing
their views on candidate or voter qualifications for the
first territorial elections until late 1956. Although the
Fabian Bureau and the Labour Party received repeated suggestions from their members concerning the issuance of an
official franchise plan, both James Griffiths and Selwyn-
Clarke believed that it would be more appropriate to wait
for the release of TANU's own proposals. In this way, the

nationalist movement and the liberal reformers could best coordinate their objectives and avoid the possibility of issuing conflicting plans.[108]

It is also clear that the liberal community played a major role in the foundation of Union policy concerning the 1958 franchise. In September, 1956, Nyerere arrived in London to request that the Colonial Office intervene and alter both the franchise proposals and the parity voting system recently endorsed by the Tanganyikan government. On September 19, the TANU chief met with Labour Party and Fabian allies in a conference hall in the House of Commons. Shortly thereafter, James Betts, the long-time friend and mentor of Nyerere, spent several weeks consulting privately with the Union leader. On October 4, Selwyn-Clarke revealed that Betts had been helping Nyerere formulate TANU demands for the 1958 elections:

> Jimmy Betts has nearly finished the memorandum working out the policy of T.A.N.U. on franchise and elections. He and I feel that this is a service we should give to Nyerere.[109]

In trying to formulate its suggestions concerning election qualifications, the Bureau sought the advice of Prof. W. J. M. Mackenzie, who had headed the territory's first constitutional commission. Mackenzie informed the liberals that the trusteeship was indeed ready to make a major political advance:

> ...I was out in Tanganyika in July...and found that things had changed a good deal (largely in the right direction) since 1952. The result is that a good deal of what I said there is obsolete so far as Tanganyika is concerned, because it is no longer necessary to be so extremely cautious there.[110]

The Bureau forwarded a copy of Mackenzie's letter to the Secretary of State, pointing out that the "obsolete" recommendations of the 1952 committee were the basis of the Government's recent franchise proposals. In response, the Fabians were informed that the Legislative Council's recent decision to approve modest reduction of income and education qualifications satisfied the need for a franchise more liberal than that originally envisioned by the Mackenzie committee.[111]

On November 7, the Bureau received a letter from Nyerere which indicated that the voter and candidate qualifications suggested by Betts had in fact been adopted as the official TANU suggestions for the coming elections. Nyerere stated:

52

Very many thanks for the help you have given me in my effort to present TANU's case here. I thank you in particular for your help in working out a detailed plan for putting our electoral and constitutional proposals into effect. The plan as it now stands is the best that we have been able to devise. I have sent a copy to TANU stating that the plan has my full support and my confidence that it will get the official support of the Union.[112]

On November 18, 1956, Rita Hinden received a letter from Chief Makwaia informing her that the proposals recently forwarded to TANU's Executive Committee by Nyerere had been approved. Thus, the Bureau clearly served in a major decision-making capacity in the formulation of TANU's demands concerning qualifications for the 1958 elections.

In December, 1956, the Fabian Bureau held its own conference to devise a policy statement on both franchise and representation in the East and Central African territories. The meeting, which was attended by most liberal reformers concerned with developments in Tanganyika, adopted a set of demands which, although somewhat vague since they were not designed for any one particular territory, nonetheless complemented the TANU proposals. Indeed, the socialist plans were in many ways more radical than those of the Africans.

The Fabian proposal advocated recognition of the fact that the British dependencies were primarily black in composition and accordingly contended that their political structures must reflect this reality. The liberals, therefore, called for the introduction of common roll elections and the creation of "geographical constituencies" in which there was "no place for special racial or tribal or minority representation."[113]

The Bureau was willing to accept a temporary system of guaranteed seats for minority groups, but refused to support any program of parity:

The most acceptable modification....as a temporary measure, is the common roll multi-member constituency with reserved seats for minorities. Where these are not practicable (for reasons of disparity in the size of the different electorates, etc.), the devices of co-option or nomination might well be used to give adequate representation to minorities. We do not favour any extension of the system of communal rolls, though its continu-

53

ance in areas where it already exists may be inevitable as an interim measure.[114]

The socialists also expressed their willingness to compromise their demands for universal adult franchise, "but only as a temporary interim measure for reasons of difficulties of electoral administration, of political bargaining, or of allowing time for the growth of African political organizations." In territories where this was necessary, the Bureau conceded that minimum educational and income qualifications could be utilized. However, the Fabians made it clear that at no time would they support the use of a multiple vote, nor would they endorse allowing voter qualifications to be left to the discretion of the territorial executive.

In summary, by 1956 the socialists had not only helped to formulate the Union's plans for territorial political development but had also devised their own general guidelines for the British dependencies of East and Central Africa. The Fabian formula was, in effect, more radical than that of TANU because of the Bureau's refusal to accept even a temporary compromise version of parity.

During the 1955-57 period the liberal and conservative factions in the home government also clashed over the banning of TANU cells. In February, 1955, Marjorie Nicholson assigned John Hynd the task of raising questions in Parliament to discover the administration's rationale behind the recent closing of TANU branches in Mwanza and Mwalampaka. She did so as the result of a direct request from Nyerere, who was concerned that the ban was the beginning of an administrative attempt to undermine the entire nationalist movement.[115]

Although Hynd attempted to initiate a debate on this issue on two separate occasions, the Secretary of State refused to discuss the matter. In April, the M.P. tried to force a confrontation by demanding that the administration take steps to identify and prosecute those individuals who were involved in the allegedly subversive activities which closed the Union cells. Lennox-Boyd refused to be led into debate and would state only that the branches had been banned "for the sake of preserving law and order" in the territory.[116] When pressed to explain additional closings in Sukumaland and Bukoba, the Secretary of State, in a written reply to the Fabian Bureau, noted that the government was convinced that there was no significant dissatisfaction in either region with official policies or administrators and that the Union had been totally banned in both areas for its attempts to create unrest where none existed. Throughout the confrontation Kambona advised the Bureau concerning the unions perception of political conditions in the regions where cells had been banned.[117]

In March, 1956, M.P. Arthur Skeffington also raised the question of the Sukumaland closings. In particular, he wished an explanation of why numerous petitions seeking permission to re-open TANU cells in the area had been denied. The Secretary of State once again refused to give specific details but did state that the individuals who presented the petitions would "most likely" disrupt the peace, and hamper the effective running of the government if the branches were given permission to resume their normal functions. Similar attempts by other liberal M.P.s to press the issue also ended in failure. The government adamantly refused to discuss the reasons behind the decision to ban any individual TANU branch. This refusal, in turn, led to angry and frustrated accusations by liberals who claimed that the Union was the victim of official persecution primarily because it effectively articulated indigenous dissatisfaction with outdated methods of British rule.

Liberal M.P.s also supported TANU in its opposition to the other political organizations which emerged during this period. In March, 1956, Eirene White and Selwyn-Clarke visited the Colonial Office and demanded an explanation of why UTP members could be allowed to serve as officials on the government side of the Legislative Council, considering the ban on civil servant political activities. In addition, they questioned the policy of selecting individuals who were chiefs as the unofficial representatives of the indigenous population.[118]

Several weeks later John Hatch and Arthur Skeffington demanded that early elections be held for Legislative Council seats, in view of the fact that the unofficial members were now, in effect, a political party. Finally, the Fabians used Venture to continuously produce articles critical of the UTP, by depicting it as a racist organization which, if allowed to thrive, would undermine the moderate policies of TANU.[119]

Liberals and conservatives also clashed on the question of economic development in the trusteeship. The Tanganyikan administration, Colonial Office, and conservative members of the home government all maintained that the economic potential of the territory was being developed in as rapid and as equitable a manner as possible. Labour Party critics, by contrast, insisted that the Colonial Development and Welfare

Acts had made only slight progress in remedying the economic maladies of the colonies. With specific reference to Tanganyika, liberals maintained that economic control was firmly in the hands of the minority community and that the system of parity only served to perpetuate this imbalance. Reformers therefore opposed both land alienation and future white settlement. In addition, they demanded that no other sectors of the economy be allowed to fall under minority control.[120] In order to partially remedy such economic inequality, they called for a major reform of the civil service system aimed at placing Africans in high level administrative posts.[121] Similarly, on June 8, 1956, Fabian Assistant Secretary Mary Winchester interviewed Lennox-Boyd and argued that a much more rapid expansion of the indigenous educational system was necessary if Africans were to gain significant employment in the territorial work force.[122]

In March, 1956, Labour M.P. Margaret Slater asked the Secretary of State to explain why Africans in Tanganyika were forced to pay a cess tax on coffee while Europeans were not. Labour demands for an official response increased when it was discovered that revenue from the tax was allocated to the Tanganyika Coffee Board, which was of far more service to European than to African growers. When the Secretary refused to offer an explanation, liberals deluged the Colonial Office with telegrams and letters of protest.

The liberal reformers, however, did not allow their ideological commitment to blind them either to the reality of conditions within the trusteeship or to the needs and capabilities of the home government. Thus, they accepted the legal justifications behind the ban on civil servant political activity. Similarly, when M.P. Fenner Brockway announced in 1956 that Tanganyika was ready for self-government, the Fabian Bureau and the Labour Party both rejected his claim as "extremely premature."[123]

In addition, the Bureau recognized that nationalist leaders in Tanganyika were often far too radical and naive in their approaches to political problems. The liberals maintained, however, that as the future leaders of the African population such individuals had to be aided. This was not done because of ideological commitment, but rather:

> ...because although we realize that they sometimes make regrettably extremist statements, we are also well aware that the discredited leaders of today may be Ministers tomorrow.[124]

When Africans in Tanganyika raised the argument that participation in the East Africa High Commission would eventually lead to federation, the Fabians denounced such apprehensions as groundless and decided to take steps to end such senseless rumors. Speaking of this problem, Selwyn-Clarke reasoned:

> The safeguards against federation are many and adequate and the African fears are absolutely groundless...As to how African suspicions can be dissipated, I would suggest that I do a paragraph for 'Venture' and that you send it for copy to the whole East African press. It would be a pity if we appear as campaigning on the matter but most educated Africans would read a statement from a friendly and unofficial source. It is better that Africans should fill their heads with their major problems that matter rather than chase an illusory will of the wisp.[125]

Finally, liberals acknowledged that the decrees of the Trusteeship Council were often based on ideological convictions which failed to take into account actual territorial conditions. Speaking of the international body, Labour Party Colonial Affairs Advisor Creech-Jones stated:

> The basic difficulty arises from the constitution of the Council. It permits representation of responsible as well as irresponsible powers, of knowledgeable as well as inexperienced members, and of the play of politics and deep prejudice.[126]

Thus, by 1957, the liberal elements of the home government and especially the Fabian socialists were committed to the support of TANU demands for political advancement and to the defense of the Union from the attacks of both the colonial administration and the conservative elements within the home government. In addition, the liberals shared many of TANU's criticisms of territorial economic and educational policies. However, neither the Fabians nor the Liberal Party operated solely on the basis of ideological conviction. Their goal was to obtain self-government for Tanganyika but to do so in a manner that took into account the realities of the territorial situation and not merely their own political preferences.

CHAPTER V

TERMINATING THE DEBATE:
CONCESSIONS AND COMPROMISE, 1958-61

Territorial Developments

Despite the numerous disagreements and unresolved issues which existed by the end of 1957, within the next four years the political situation in Tanganyika was to undergo series of major transformations which by 1961 would result in the creation of an African majority government.

The alterations which occurred in Britain's longstanding policies were to a great extent due to changes in key administrative personnel. On July 7, 1958, Sir Richard Turnbull replaced Edward Twining as Governor of Tanganyika. The new Governor greatly reduced the tense atmosphere with the territory by publicly articulating his faith in Nyerere's ability to maintain a moderate and cooperative course of action in his dealings with the administration.

Another major change in colonial personnel occurred in the home government in October, 1959, when Ian MacLeod replaced Lennox-Boyd as Secretary of State for the Colonies. MacLeod believed that the Crown territories should be transformed into self-governing members of the Commonwealth as rapidly as possible. He was convinced that the moderate philosophy of Nyerere made it possible to initiate rapid and far-reaching changes in the political structure of the trusteeship.[127]

Relations between the administration and the nationalists improved markedly in the 1958-59 period, as the government initiated a series of far reaching changes into the dependency's political structure. Key among these alterations was the conduction of the first territorial elections which were divided into two phases, each involving five voting districts. The elections were based on a limited franchise and a common electoral roll. One candidate of each race was to be elected in each constituency. In the first phase of the elections TANU candidates and Asians and Europeans endorsed by the Union won all 15 seats.

As a result of the sweeping nationalist victory, only three contenders came forward to challenge the Union during the second phase of the elections. Once again TANU and her approved non African candidates captured all 15 seats.

When it became clear early in the campaigning that the Union was going to sweep the elections, the Governor opted to announce a number of dramatic constitutional changes. In an address before the legislature, Turnbull acknowledged that the Crown accepted the inevitability of an African controlled government and announced the administration's intention to allow unofficial members to serve as ministers for the first time.

Furthermore, in May, 1959, Turnbull created a Post Elections Committee, charged with the responsibility of investigating possible substitutions for the parity system and with formulating new voter and candidate qualifications for the next territorial elections. The committee ultimately recommended the abolition of both parity representation and the tripartite vote. In their place, it suggested the use of "open seats," i.e., a position to which a member of any race could be elected for most constituencies. Substantial reductions in both voter and candidate qualifications for the Legislative Council were also suggested.

The Governor addressed the territorial legislature on December 15 and announced the acceptance of the Post Elections Committee's suggestions. Turnbull revealed that a general election would be held in September, 1960, to create an unofficial majority in the Legislative Council. More significantly, he announced that the recently established Council of Ministers would be reorganized to give numerical superiority to non-officials. This alteration, in effect, promised TANU internal control of the government.

During the period 1960-61 the pace of constitutional advancement in the territory accelerated even more rapidly. On April 26, 1960, the government announced plans for far reaching changes in the executive branch. Primary among these was the creation of the post of Chief Minister, who would serve as the Governor's key advisor and as the Leader of Government Business within the legislature. This post was to be filled by an elected member of the Legislative Council.

In addition, the executive alterations called for the formation of a new Council of Ministers to be comprised of the Governor (who was to serve as Council president), the Deputy Governor, ten unofficial ministers and two Civil Service ministers. The alterations amounted to a guarantee that internal self government would be initiated following the 1960 election.

TANU and the European and Asian candidates it endorsed were able to capture all but one of the 71 seats in the Legislative Council.

Shortly thereafter, the Governor announced that Julius Nyerere had been chosen to serve as Chief Minister. Appoint-

ments to the remaining ministerial posts were made to 6
Africans, 1 Asian, and 2 Europeans. All of the selections
were made by Turnbull during a series of private consulta-
tions with Nyerere. The power of executive initiative was
now in the hands of nationalists.

The governor also announced that a Constitutional
Conference would take place in March, 1961, to plan the
final steps necessary to grant Tanganyika full independence.
It required only three days of deliberation to agree that
full internal self-government would be initiated on May 1,
1960, with independence day to be scheduled for that
December.

The Minority Communities: The End of Political Influence
As the first territorial elections approached, most
members of the immigrant communities chose to avoid political
participation, realizing that under the new electoral system
they could little effect the course of territorial development because of their small numbers.

The only recognized party representing white settler
opinion, the UTP, was devastated in the territorial elections. So decisive was its defeat that by December, 1958,
the UTP ceased to have any significant function within the
trusteeship.

As a whole, the Asian community of Tanganyika continued
to avoid participation in territorial politics. However,
the more progressive elements of the immigrant race did
follow the leadership of the Asian Association which closely
allied itself with TANU plans for constitutional development.
Its three principal leaders, Amir H. Jamal, S. Mustafa and
M.N. Rattansey all campaigned for the Union. In return,
they received TANU endorsement and enjoyed a wide margin of
victory in their constituencies.

The United Nations: Final Considerations
During the 1960-61 period the question of territorial
political evolution ceased to be a source of major controversy within the Trusteeship Council. The general attitude
within the international body was one of satisfaction with
the rapid political changes initiated by the Administering
Authority.

On April 21, 1961, the General Assembly passed a resolution calling for the termination of the Trusteeship
Agreement, to take effect immediately after the granting of
independence by the Crown. This recommendation was officially activated by a unanimous vote of the Security Council on
December 14, 1961.

The Nationalist Movement: Protest and Victory
The period 1958-61 was marked by the peaceful achievement of all of TANU's demands for territorial political
reform. Nevertheless, the territory continued to be the site
of repeated instances of local unrest. The most troublesome
area was once again Sukumaland and in particular the district
of Geita.

The Geita crisis began in March, 1958, when the government announced the creation of a multi-racial district
council based on parity representation. Local TANU leaders
angrily protested the government action, complaining that
only the chiefs and not the people had been consulted in
this decision.

Several unauthorized massive demonstrations followed in
the wake of the TANU protests. When a visit by Nyerere
produced a great rush of new membership for the Union, the
government invoked the Incitement to Violence Act to ban all
TANU connected activities in Geita for a six month period.

Despite the ban popular demonstrations continued.
Crowds up to 1,000 would picket daily before the local
administrative headquarters and the repeated arrest of
demonstration leaders failed to quell the unrest.

On July 29 a crowd of some 3,000 to 5,000 persons
marched to the office of the Provincial Commissioner and
demanded that the ban on TANU be lifted. After camping in a
nearby sports field for three days, the crowd was dispersed
by the use of tear gas. On August 11 a similar incident
occurred.

The crisis in Geita produced a personal confrontation
between Nyerere and the administration. In July, 1958, the
TANU leader was formally charged with three counts of
sedition, resulting from his denunciation of the Geita
District Commissioner in a recent edition of Sauti Ya Tanu.
The TANU President pleaded innocent to the charges but was
convicted and fined 150 pounds.

Clearly, the major task facing the Union in these years
involved participation in the territorial elections. The
TANU platform for the 1958-59 contests called for a majority
of elected ministers by 1959, an end to parity via the
creation of an elected African majority in the Legislative
Council, single member constituencies based on district
boundaries; the abolition of the compulsory tripartite
voting system and the initiation of a territory-wide program
of free and compulsory primary education. The Union was
most adamant in its demand for the termination of the
qualitative franchise. In its place TANU called for the
initiation of universal adult suffrage.[128]

62

When the final version of the Ramage Report was announced in the Legislative Council on December 15, Nyerere declared that the Union would accept all of the government proposals. He did, however, record his objection to the maintenance of literacy and income qualifications for the franchise.

The Home Government: The Culmination of Fabian Involvement

The period 1958-61 was marked by a radical decline of tensions within the home government concerning the question of Tanganyikan political development. The concessions granted by the Crown, coupled with the influx of more moderate administrators in both the Colonial Office and the territorial government resulted in the equitable solution of most of the major sources of conflict. Nonetheless, the liberal and conservative factions remained ideologically divided in their appraisal of events within the trusteeship and in their basic attitudes toward the concept of colonialism.

As has been noted between 1958 and 1959 a major transformation occurred in both Colonial Office personnel and policies. The expenses involved in attempting to advance the social and economic systems of the dependencies at the same pace as the political sector had resulted in the bankruptcy of the Colonial Development Corporation and its multifold subsidiary agencies. Gradually, the home government recognized the impossibility of continuing to bear the burden of such rapid internal expansion.

Labour and Conservative M.P.'s, nonetheless, remained divided in their reaction to the rapidly changing events on the African continent. The more conservative elements looked upon the increasingly successful nationalist movements with skepticism and demanded safeguards to protect British subjects and investments. Accordingly, they supported such policies as the multiple-vote, the qualitative franchise and the retention of official majorities. At the same time, they pointed with pride to the economic and social advances which came as a result of the colonial experience, arguing that British rule had indeed made great efforts to prepare the sub-Saharan territories for participation in the community of nations.

Liberals, by contrast, argued that the pace of political development should continue to accelerate until all of the dependencies had attained self-rule, either within or outside of the Commonwealth. Furthermore, they maintained that while it was necessary for the Crown to help develop the economic and educational systems of the colonies, such aid should in no way impede the pace of political evolution. Claiming that direct and immediate participation in modern political activities was the only viable means of developing stable regimes, liberals called for rapid advancement toward self-rule and for long range economic assistance from the Crown after independence.[129]

With specific reference to Tanganyika, the more conservative interests within both the Conservative Party and the Colonial Office complained that far too many concessions were being granted to Nyerere. Coupled with this complaint was the often repeated accusation that the home government had been pressured into speeding the pace of constitutional development by liberals within Great Britain and by the enemies of Britain on the Trusteeship Council.

Liberals countered with the argument that the Nyerere regime should be given immediate control of an independent African majority government which recognized no special privileges or guarantees for the immigrant communities. They also called for the initiation of universal adult suffrage and for the termination of indirect rule at all administrative levels.

While the period was devoid of major confrontations, the liberal factions within Britain, and especially the Fabian socialists, nonetheless maintained a keen interest in Tanganyikan affairs. As such, they stood prepared to offer TANU guidance, moral support, and publicity whenever the need arose. At the same time, they carefully scrutinized the many constitutional changes occurring within the trusteeship to ensure that they did indeed conform to the aspirations of the nationalists.

Thus, the period 1958-61 was marked by a continued spirit of close cooperation between TANU and her supporters in the home government. As the pace of political activity became less frantic, the socialists began to alter the scope of their propaganda campaigns. Instead of stressing the inadequacies of British colonial rule and the necessity of constitutional advances, their speeches and literature now emphasized the stability and reasonableness of the emerging African regimes and the necessity of increased economic aid from Great Britain. While the aim of earlier publicity had been to defend struggling African political organizations from reactionary resistance, the literature and speeches of this period heralded the victory of African nationalism and the promise of a prosperous Commonwealth of freely participating independent states.

During these years, key leaders of the Tanganyika nationalist drive frequently appeared before liberal reform groups to outline their plans for territorial development. From 1958 to 1959 Nyerere and his chief lieutenants presented more than twenty well publicized speeches to members of the Fabian Society and to factions within the Labour Party.[130] The liberals also produced a substantial amount of literature concerning developments within the territory. The Fabian Society utilized Venture to carefully explain and endorse the TANU platform during the 1958-59 elections. Realizing that there was considerable public concern within the home government over the future of minority groups under African dominated regimes, the socialists persuaded Nyerere to write a number of articles in which he stressed TANU's opposition to racism. At the same time, the Bureau convinced prominent members of the territory's minority groups to issue statements in which they affirmed their trust in TANU's moderate policies.[131] Similarly, extensive publicity was generated concerning both the Union's electoral victory and its willingness to accept a compromise on the question of constitutional change. The socialist literature stressed the fact that TANU did indeed enjoy a mandate from the territorial population and that it represented a moderate, well-balanced approach to the goal of self government. The reformers also provided widespread publicity for the political writings of the nationalists. For example, Nyerere's Barriers to Democracy was produced in capsule form by both the Fabian Society and the Labour Party. In addition, M.P. Arthur Skeffington wrote a widely distributed pamphlet entitled Tanganyika in Transition in which he provided an historical survey and ideological defense of the nationalist movement. The pamphlet was conceived by Selwyn-Clarke in close consultation with both Nyerere and Kambona. This was done to enhance the image of TANU within Britain in the hope of gaining substantial economic aid for territorial development after independence.[132] The Fabians alone produced no fewer than 12 pamphlets and 47 major articles in support of the Nyerere regime during the 1959-1961 period.

Throughout this phase of rapid political transformation, the Fabian Bureau also maintained a steady stream of correspondence with key personalities within the territory and consistently encouraged them to make public statements of support for TANU both within Tanganyika and before the press in the home government. Over 300 members of the ninety communities engaged in such correspondence with the Bureau.[133]

The socialists, realizing that TANU had successfully achieved most of her major goals, were especially eager to assist the Union in speeding the territory's advancement toward complete independence and in gaining substantial economic aid for internal development projects. This attitude was well expressed by Selwyn-Clarke in a letter to the Executive Committee of TANU:

We are of course delighted with the constitutional alterations and the promise of self-government for the next year.

Any concrete information that you may have on further needs which should get support from this country, if you will let me know, our M.P.'s will certainly take up your points. We are in fact seeking an adjournment debate on economic conditions in Tanganyika.[134]

The liberal community carefully monitored the rapid pace of political development between 1958 and 1959 in order to assist TANU in any way possible. In May, 1957, the Labour Party sent a delegation headed by M.P. James Callahan to the Colonial Office to demand that the government issue a final policy statement concerning the date and structure of the proposed territorial elections.[135] In the months that followed, the liberals made repeated attempts to effect a modification in the election plans which would complement TANU's demands for the termination of the parity system. The Colonial Secretary however refused to consider such proposals.

Similarly, when the date for the 1960 territorial elections was announced M.P. James Johnson called upon the government to allocate special funds for adult education within the African community, to better prepare blacks for participation in the electoral process.[136] The Fabian Bureau also conducted an investigation into voter skills and upon discovering the lack of political understanding which existed in the more backward regions of the territory, demanded the creation of district level voter training programs.[137]

The socialists consistently rallied to the defense of TANU whenever Union cells came under administrative censure. On March 3, Arthur Skeffington raised before Parliament the question of recent closings of the party headquarters in Iringa. The Secretary of State, however, refused to provide details concerning the decision to ban TANU in that district. When repeated attempts by M.P.s failed to produce a more elaborate explanation, the Labour Party, at the request of the Fabian Bureau, sent a delegation to Lennox-Boyd and complained that the territorial administration was attempting to undermine TANU. They utilized Nyerere's often repeated argument that all Union members in the banned districts were being denied their right of political participation because of the crimes of a few individuals.[138]

When continued complaints concerning African dissatisfaction with official agricultural policies came to the attention of liberals in the home government, the Fabian Bureau despatched Arthur Gaitskell, an expert on soil conservation, to investigate conditions in the troubled areas.[139] During the same year, John Hynd demanded an explanation concerning the removal of Tanganyikan Africans from the Matagoro hills which had forced a number of traditional groups to abandon their tribal land holdings. When Lennox-Boyd justified the removals as a necessary part of a long-range government irrigation project, the Fabians assigned Marjorie Nicholson to investigate the incident. Although in both cases it was concluded that the government actions were justified, the keen interest manifested by the socialists was a reflection of liberal determination to continue to act as the ally and defender of the African nationalists.

For all practical purposes, however, the battle between the liberal and conservative factions concerning the political future of Tanganyika was a dead issue. Typical of this new feeling was Nyerere's remark to James Betts "We can now afford to be slow about something."[140] A jubilant Amir Jamal reported to his Fabian allies "We are all fighting the same battle now. The race is run, and the help rendered by you and other friends in the U.K. cannot easily be measured in words."[141]

During the period of 1960-61 developments in Tanganyika contributed little to the perpetuation of the ideological conflicts within the British Government. As the period of British control drew to a close, however, liberal and conservative factions differed in their evaluations of the role played by the Crown within the trusteeship. The Conservative party and the Colonial Office viewed the emancipation of Tanganyika as the result of a carefully planned program of political training initiated by the home government, part of which had included a well formulated system of economic and educational advancement resulting from the concentrated efforts of the Colonial Development Corporation. The liberals, by contrast, maintained that territorial independence had come as the result of persistent efforts on the part of the nationalist movement, which had received little

more than opposition from the Colonial Office and the right
wing faction in Parliament. They historically evaluated the
British systems of indirect rule and parity as totally
inadequate failures which had produced unnecessary impedi-
ments to the emerging sense of indigenous political awareness. The liberals, consequently, demanded substantial
financial aid for post-independence development to partially
compensate for the inadequacies of colonial rule.

During the 1960-61 period, correspondence between the
liberal activist groups and TANU decreased markedly. With
virtually all of the Union's aspirations achieved, there
were few problems with which the socialist organization
could assist the nationalists. The Fabian Bureau and the
Liberal Party did however continue to support TANU in every
way possible. Thus, when the question of financial aid to
the independent government arose, liberals sent a delegation
to the Secretary of State to demand that funds originally
allocated for long-range trusteeship development be released
to the Tanganyikan government.[142]

Similarly, when Nyerere decided to amend the TANU
constitution to fit the needs of the independent government,
he sought the advice of Fabian political experts and
ultimately modeled the new constitution on the Labour Party
Contract.[143] Thus the liberal factions and especially the
Fabians continued to function as the mentors and supporters
of TANU until the eve of independence.

CHAPTER VI

CONCLUSION

An historical analysis of developments within Tanganyika during the years 1946-61 reveals that the political evolution of the trusteeship was the result of a number of interrelated forces each operating within its own frame of reference toward its own specific goals.

Key among these factors was the British administration, which, until 1960, enjoyed the power of initiative in matters involving territorial development. Although always recognizing the fact that Tanganyika would ultimately have a black majority government, the British Colonial Office nonetheless viewed this transformation as a long-range process which would have to be preceded by substantial advances in the social, economic and educational sectors of the trusteeship.

At the same time, Crown policy stressed the protection of the European and Asian minority communities whom it viewed as the only potential sources of internal assistance in this development effort. It was because of this view that the system of minority protection referred to as "parity" was introduced.

Within Tanganyika, Crown policy was ardently supported by the white settler community who feared that self-rule would mean the loss of their political, economic, and social privileges. The majority of the members of the Asian community, by contrast, avoided participation in the controversial battles of the post-war years. Those few individuals who did enter the political arena, however, became the supporters of the nationalist movement. This decision came largely as the result of the strong ties which progressive Asians maintained with the Fabian Bureau in Britain.

Undoubtedly the most active of all groups concerned with the question of territorial political development was the African nationalist movement. By the early 1950's, blacks had become aware that the milder forms of political activity employed by the early indigenous associations contributed little to the acceleration of territorial political development. With the advent of Julius Nyerere to the presidency of TANU, the African population had the organizational means of successfully challenging British plans for territorial evolution and of mobilizing their demands for an independent black majority government.

The Trusteeship Council of the United Nations was also a major participant in the debate over territorial political

69

development. From its inception, the international body was sharply divided between the colonial powers and the anti-imperialist factions, in the Trusteeship Council and the General Assembly. Accordingly, the annual reports of the Administering Authority, the findings of the visiting mission teams and the petitions received from the territorial inhabitants all became weapons in an ideological battle and were not effectively utilized as evidence upon which to formulate a realistic appraisal of the territorial situation.

The course of political evolution within the Trusteeship was, unquestionably, also greatly influenced by events within the home government. Throughout the period 1946-61, the liberal and conservative factions were divided in their view concerning the pace and structure of territorial development.

The conservatives insisted that substantial economic and educational advancement would have to precede any significant political change. They firmly believed that a gradual program of overall development extended over several generations would have to precede the initiation of responsible government.

At the opposite end of the political spectrum were the liberal reformers, represented primarily by the Fabian Colonial Bureau, who demanded a rapid pace of political development for Tanganyika. It was their position that the initiation of self-government would have to be given top priority, even if constitutional development far outdistanced changes in the territory's social, economic and educational structure. By applying pressure on the Colonial Office through their representatives in Parliament, these activists were repeatedly able to bring the issue of Tanganyikan political evolution to the attention of the British public. So interested in the territory were the socialists that their active involvement actually predated that of the nationalists.

In their attempts to stir public interest, the socialists employed the floors of Parliament, the friendly press, public speeches, discussion groups and an endless barrage of pamphlets, leaflets, broadsheets and magazine articles to spread their message. Such forms of publicity were generally highly critical of British administrative policy and at the same time stressed the reasonableness and moderation of TANU. Thus, the reformers appealed for the support of not only the liberal, but also the more moderate elements within the home government. At the same time they maintained close contacts with TANU leaders and with sympathetic members of the territory's non-African population. However, the Fabians did consistently attempt to evaluate developments within the territory on their factual merit and not on the basis of their own ideological preferences. Accordingly, at key times they were willing to support administrative policies that were unpopular with the nationalists.

Finally, the papers of liberal reformers clearly revealed the strong influence which the Fabians had within TANU itself. The early political training of Nyerere was largely at the hands of Bureau mentors. Throughout the independence drive the Society served as both the advisor and defender of many of the leading Union spokesmen. In addition it actually helped to formulate TANU policy on critical political questions. Clearly, the liberal elements of the home government were key participators in the drive for Tanganyikan independence and a force of moderation and compromise in a confrontation situation where the other actors were far more polarized in their views. Thus they may be credited with much of the peaceful compromise which allowed Tanganyika to achieve independence in a reasonable and balanced manner.

1. In speaking of members of either the Executive or Legislative Councils, the term "official" refers to members who were colonial service personnel; "unofficial" members were not employed by the colonial administation; "nominated" members were either officials or unofficials and were appointed by the Governor to represent important groups or interests; "elected" members represented electoral constituencies in the legislature.

2. P.A. Emerson, "Introduction to the File Listings of the Fabian Colonial Bureau Papers," Rhodes House Africana Collection, Oxford, England. Emerson's introduction offers a comprehensive study of the Fabian Bureau's philosophy and activities. The complete records of the Fabian Colonial Bureau (hereafter referred to as FCB) are held in Rhodes House. This Research Center serves as the principal British archive dedicated to the collection of primary source material on all aspects of Great Britain's African dependencies.

3. List of M.P.s, denoting their "fields of concentration," dated February, 1955, in the miscellaneous notes and paper files, FCB papers. The list is in the handwriting of Fabian Secretary Marjorie Nicholson. The M.P.s so noted were: Fenner Brockway, Harold Davies, Rt. Hon. Hilary Marquand, Sir Leslie Plummer, W. T. Proctor, Eirene White, W. Tom Williams, Lord Farington, and the Earl of Listowel. John Hynd was designated as an expert on Tanganyikan constitutional problems, and along with Eirene White shared the designation as an expert on race relations within the territory.

4. Hinden to Arthur Creech-Jones, June 22, 1942 FCB papers.

5. Arthur Creech-Jones was born in Britain in 1891. Educated at Whitehall Boys School, he joined the War Office as a clerk on the clerical staff in January 1907. His first exposure to liberal politics came in 1908 when he joined the Dulwich Branch of the League of Progressive Thought and Services. By 1910 he was Secretary of the branch and an active organizer in the Borough of Camberwell Trade and Labour Council. He

served as Secretary of the latter from 1913-22. In 1914 he joined the London Egyptian Debating Society and gave frequent lectures on socialism and nationalism. It was here that he made lasting contact with key socialist leaders, including Herbert Morrison, James Mylles and Fenner Brockway. During World War I, Creech-Jones was imprisoned for refusing to serve in the armed forces. Upon his release in 1919 he served as National Secretary of the Transport and General Workers Union and from 1921-28 was an executive member of the London Labour Party. After an unsuccessful bid for public office in 1929 he was elected to the House of Commons as Labour Party candidate for Shipley Division, Yorkshire in 1935. He retained this seat until 1950 when realignment of the district led to his defeat. From 1925-40 he served on the Executive Committee of the Fabian Society and in 1940 became Chairman of the Colonial Bureau. He served as a member of the Labour Party Imperial Advisory Committee and during World War Two played a key role in the formation of the party's colonial policies. He was the initiator of the plan to end colonial rule and to form a Commonwealth of freely participating states. It was he who planned and established the Colonial Development Corporation. Based on "Introduction to the Guide to the Papers of Arthur Creech-Jones", Rhodes House. The archive holds the entire collection of Creech-Jones' public papers. Hereafter referred to as "Creech-Jones papers."

6. "Draft of a Speech by Secretary of State Arthur Creech-Jones for the General meeting of the Labour Party, April 1946", in "Labour Party Policies" file, Creech-Jones papers.

7. The necessity of maintaining this balance and the problems encountered in attempting to do so are reflected in the copious socialist writings of the period. Representative examples include: James Griffiths, Arthur Creech-Jones. and Rita Hinden, The Way Forward, London: Fabian Publications Ltd., 1950; Rita Hinden, Common Sense and Colonial Development, London: Fabian Publications Ltd., 1949 and Socialists and the Empire, London: Fabian Publications Ltd., 1947; Arthur Creech-Jones, "A Labour View of British Colonial Policy," United Empire, Vol. XXXVI, No. 4 (July-August 1945), 127-131 and Labour's Colonial Policy, London: Fabian

Publications Ltd., 1947; L. Silberman, Crisis in Africa, London: Fabian Publications Ltd., 1947.

8. William Malcom Hailey, Native Administration in the British African Territories, Vol. II, London: H.M.S.O., 1950, p. 352.

9. Tanganyika, Report of the Committee on Constitutional Development, Dar es Salaam: The Government Printer, 1951, p. 7.

10. The term "parity" refers to the establishment of an equal number of representatives from each of the three racial communities.

11. The term "alienation" refers to the reservation of designated plots of land for the use of the government or individuals granted right of domain. Although land could be claimed which was previously held by residents of any race, in practice it was always African held land which was designated for reservation. The Government was responsible for the compensation and resettlement of persons removed from alienated lands.

12. Letter from H. K. B. Mwapachu, a black in the Social Welfare Department, Tanganyika, to Hinden, December 4, 1950, FCB papers. Because of the animosity of the white community, Mwapachu refused to contribute articles on territorial events to Venture, the Fabian journal. Similar reasons caused Thomas Marealle, Paramount Chief of the Wachagga, member of the Legislative Council, and a dedicated socialist, from publicly expressing his views. Marealle file, FCB papers.

13. Under the "communal roll" system, each racial group voted separately and only for members of its own race.

14. "Common roll" referred to the use of a single list of candidates in which no racial distinctions were made. Voters were not required to cast ballots only for members of their own race, nor were they required to vote for a specific number of candidates from each racial community. Central Muslim Association, minutes of meeting held July 29, 1950, Dar es Salaam. Tanganyika Territorial files, "Political Activities, 1945-54," FCB papers.

15. United Nations, Report of the Visiting Mission, 1948, Appendix 1.

16. Hinden letter of July 18, 1945, FCB papers.

17. Letter from Hinden to S. M. Mtengeti, August 18, 1948, FCB papers. Mtengeti, a black activist in Tanganyika, requested the names of M.P.s who were interested in helping to advance the pace of constitutional development in the territory. In reply, Hinden supplied the names of F. Skinnard, John Rankin, J. Hynd, and Reginald Sorinsen.

18. "Problems Arising in Connection with Tanganyika"; notes on controversial issues drawn up by the FCB, 1945-50 Tanganyika files, FCB papers.

19. "Notes on Tanganyika, 1948" Rita Hinden correspondence files, FCB papers.

20. Letter from Lord Ammon to Hinden, January 12, 1945, FCB papers.

21. Hinden to Dugdale, March 14, 1945, Creech-Jones papers.

22. Great Britain, Colonial Office, Col. No. 193, Labour Conditions in East Africa, London: His Majesty's Stationery Office, 1946, paras. 170-194.

23. Great Britain, Parliament, Parliamentary Debates, House of Lords, May 11, 1949, col's 541-592.

24. Hinden to James Johnson, M.P., April 18, 1950, FCB papers.

25. Notes of a meeting with Conservative delegation, February 2, 1949, Creech-Jones papers.

26. Creech-Jones to FCB, February 6, 8, 1949, Creech-Jones papers.

27. The year 1950 found Creech-Jones out of office due to the reapportionment of his district. He was replaced by James Griffiths, a liberal with socialist leanings, who nonetheless proved to be another unexpected thorn in the side of the FCB. Rita Hinden to Secretary of State Griffiths, June 29, 1950, FCB papers.

76

28. Griffiths to Hinden, October 20, 1950, FCB papers.

29. Marjorie Nicholson to Captain Charles Smith, May 19, 1946, FCB papers.

30. Hinden to the Secretary of State for the Colonies, October 29, 1946, FCB papers.

31. Griffiths to Hinden, October 20, 1950, FCB papers.

32. Nicholson files, "Land Policy, Tanganyika," FCB papers. This single incident resulted in the production of three Fabian tracts on the East African land problem, four interviews with the Secretary of State and over a dozen questions on the floor of commons.

33. Correspondence between FCB and Kenneth Younger, M.P., April-June 1946, FCB papers.

34. Hinden, notes for an article entitled "Tanganyika Tangle," Hinden files 1950, FCB papers.

35. Based on the files of M.P.s Kenneth Younger and J. Skinnard, which contain listings of the numerous questions asked by each in the 1945-50 period concerning territorial political development FCB papers.

36. Notes on "Political Advancement in the East African Territories," Tanganyika territorial files, 1948-49, Creech-Jones papers.

37. FCB notes on "Constitutional Policy in Tanganyika," April, 1950, FCB papers.

38. Hinden, "Tanganyika notes," April, 1950, FCB papers.

39. Notes on "Constitutional Policy," FCB papers.

40. Nicholson, Notes on East African policy, Spring 1950, FCB papers.

41. "Notes on a meeting at Transport House," April 17, 1950, FCB papers.

42. Nicholson, "Notes on Tanganyika Policy," April 23, 1950, FCB papers.

43. Correspondence between Nicholson and Dr. Kenneth Little of the London School of Economics, April 17-23, 1950, FCB papers.

44. Nicholson to Makwaia, August 3-11, 1950, FCB papers.

45. "T.A.A. correspondence files," FCB papers. See especially Nicholson to Marealle, November 14, 1950; Hinden to Marealle, March 31, 1950 and Makwaia-Hinden correspondence, October 1949-April 1950.

46. Tanganyika Territory, Legislative Council, Ordinance No. 11, 1954, Dar es Salaam: The Government Printer, 1954, pp. 1-2.

47. The term "responsible" was used to designate a government of elected representatives, headed by a Prime Minister and a ministerial cabinet. Responsible government did not, however, necessitate independence, i.e., separation from the authority of the Crown. Tanganyika, Constitutional Development Commission, Report of the Special Commissioner Appointed to Examine Matters Arising Out of the Report of the Committee on Constitutional Development, Dar es Salaam: The Government Printer, 1953, pp. 1-4.

48. United Nations, Trusteeship Council, Official Records, "Petitions from Tanganyika," T/Pet. 2/118 and 2/103, August and October, 1951.

49. United Nations, Trusteeship Council, Report of the Visiting Mission 1954, pp. 12-15.

50. Julius Kambarage Nyerere. Born in 1922 at Buliama, Julius was the eldest son of chief Nyerere Burito of the Wazanaki. At the age of twelve Nyerere was sent to a mission school at Musoma, where he was baptized a Roman Catholic in 1934. After three years of elementary education he was sent to Tabora where he completed Standard X. Nyerere attended Makerere College from 1943-45 and obtained a diploma in Education. Following graduation he was employed as an instructor in St. Mary's Catholic School near Tabora. In 1949 Nyerere departed for Edinburgh where he earned a doctorate in economics. Throughout his graduate years, Nyerere maintained constant contact with Fabian headquarters.

He exchanged theories on African political development with Nicholson and Hinden and contributed several articles to Venture. Upon his return to Tanganyika in 1952, Nyerere became active in territorial politics and joined the T.A.A. in 1952. His education and travel, coupled with his charismatic speaking and leadership ability led to his election as President of the Association in 1953.

51. United Nations, Trusteeship Council, Trusteeship Council Resolution 468 (XI), A/2150, pp. 49-50.

52. United Nations, Trusteeship Council, Official Records, 11th Session, 438th Meeting (1954), p. 26.

53. Hinden to Hatch, June 20, 1950, FCB papers.

54. Hinden to Labour M.P.s, June 8, 1951; Labour Party Political Education Service, Discussion Notes No. 25, British Africa, London: The Labour Party, April, 1950.

55. Hynd-Nicholson correspondence, April 19 - July 13, 1951, FCB papers.

56. Venture, Vol. 13, No. 9 (October 1951), 1.

57. Betts-Nicholson correspondence concerning Nyerere, November 1953-August 1954, FCB papers. The files of the Fabian Colonial Bureau reveal that members of the society had helped Nyerere during his student days by editing one of his early manuscripts concerning race relations in East Africa. They also frequently advised him of the legal complications involved in various plans he put forward for territorial development. Finally, the Fabians had tutored him in the arts of research, debate and polemics.

58. Nicholson to Mwapachu Office, July 14, 1954, FCB papers.

59. Johnson to Hinden, February 6, 1951, FCB papers.

60. The May debate was initiated by M. P. Hynd, and the February 1954 controversy was introduced by James Johnson. Rita Hinden papers, M.P. files, FCB papers.

61. Hinden-Nicholsen correspondence, May 23 - June 4, 1954, FCB papers.

62. Nicholson to FCB, March 3, 8, 14, 1954. See also her report in Venture, Vol. 6 No. 1 (May 1954) 4-5.

63. Hynd to Creech-Jones, March 24, 25, 28, 1954, Creech-Jones papers; Nicholson to Hynd, April 20, 1954, FCB papers.

64. Hinden to John Rankin, M.P., January 29, 1951; Hinden to Dr. Ralph Bunche, September 27, 1950, FCB papers. See also Margery Perham's article in The Listener, December 30, 1954.

65. Selwyn-Clarke to J. H. Lodge, May 27, 1951, FCB papers.

66. Arthur Creech-Jones, "What is Partnership?" (a mimeographed policy paper widely circulated by the liberal reform groups, 1951-52); "British Colonial Policy with Reference to Africa," International Affairs, Vol. XXIV, No. 3 (August 1951), 151-164.

67. Creech-Jones to Labour M.P.s, February 6, 1952, Creech-Jones papers.

68. This analysis of the Fabian Bureau's position is based on the proceedings of their Symposium on Partnerhsip and Political Development held in Manchester, March 23-29, 1952; FCB and Creech-Jones papers.

69. A. M. Tobias to Hinden, April 30, 1954, FCB papers.

70. Nicholson to Tobias, July 14, 1954, FCB papers.

71. East Africa and Rhodesia editorials, June-July, 1954. The Labour Party, by contrast, supported African demands to end forced agricultural procedures at its policy-making convention at Scarborough, July 23-27, 1954. Labour Party Archives, Labour Headquarters, Transport House, London.

72. Munanka to Nicholson, July 27, 1954, FCB papers.

73. Nicholson to FCB Advisory Committee, September 3, 1954, FCB papers.

74. Kambona to Nicholson, February 27, 1956, FCB papers.

75. Nyerere, in a letter to Nicholson stated that "The few truly active Asians tend to be sympathetic to Union designs", April 22, 1956, FCB papers. Hinden noted that by 1956 the FCB was engaged in regular correspondence with nine prominent Asian community leaders. "Notes on Political Developments--Tanganyika, 1956," FCB papers.

76. Nyerere to Creech-Jones, December 22, 1957, Creech-Jones papers.

77. Nyerere press statement outlining TANU demands for constitutional reform, October 1956, TANU files, FCB papers.

78. Selwyn-Clarke-Nyerere correspondence, March 10-16, 1957, FCB papers.

79. Trusteeship Council Records, March 24, 1955, pp. 271-273.

80. United Nations Document T/PV. 820, p. 28.

81. United Nations News, (No. 16/56), April 12, 1956.

82. Nicholson notes on "Conditions in Tanganyika", October 3, 1955, FCB papers.

83. Selwyn-Clarke to Lennox-Boyd, April 6, 1955, FCB papers.

84. Selwyn-Clarke to Lennox-Boyd, April 22, 1955, FCB papers. The Fabian Secretary criticized the Crown's rebuttal to the 1954 Visiting Mission proposals. The administration had specifically denied that a viable nationalist organization existed within the trusteeship. See: Report of the 1954 Visiting Mission: Observations of the Administering Authority (Dar es Salaam: The Government Printer, 1955), passim.

85. Hatch to Colonial Office, February 3, 1956, Labour Party Archives.

86. Nyerere to Nicholson, March 23, 1955, FCB papers.

87. Betts to Nyerere, September 3, 1955; Selwyn-Clarke to Arthur Skeffington, M. P., September 17-18, 1956, FCB papers.

88. Kambona files 1952-1962 FCB papers.

89. D. F. Heath to Betts, August 19, 1957, Betts files, Labour Party Archives.

90. Kambona to Secretary, FCB, October 18, 1955, FCB papers. Kambona reported that "There followed a rush of membership in his wake".

91. By July, 1957 the Bureau corresponded with over 80 members of the non-African communities. Selwyn-Clarke "Notes on Tanganyika", July, 1957 FCB papers.

92. Hatch to Secretary of State, September 8, 1955, Lennox-Boyd files, Conservative Party Headquarters.

93. Nicholson to Nyerere, September 23, 1955, FCB papers.

94. Selwyn-Clarke to Hynd, March 18, 1955, Labour Party Archives.

95. See John Hynd's condemnation in Parliamentary Debates (House of Commons) 5th ses., Vol. 582 (December 7, 1955), cols. 65-66.

96. Kambona interview, February 9, 1956, FCB papers.

97. Parliamentary Debates (House of Commons), 5th ses., Vol. 582 (February 22, 1956), col. 121. It should be noted that these very questions were suggested by Kambona in a meeting with Labour M.P.s at Transport House on February 16, 1956. Labour Party Archives.

98. Winchester to Hynd and White, February 18, 1956, FCB papers.

99. Parliamentary Debates (House of Commons) 5th ses., Vol. 582 (February 28, March 1, 1956), cols. 1121 and 1206.

100. Selwyn-Clarke to Lennox-Boyd, April 6, 1955, Labour Party Archives.

101. Minutes of Working Committee Meeting, June 28, 1956, FCB papers.

102. Resolution adopted at the British Labour Party Annual Conference at Blackpool, October, 1956, Labour Party Archives.

103. Text of Griffiths message to Labour M.P.s, November 11, 1956, Labour Party Archives.

104. Griffiths assigned White this task on October 23, 1956 Labour Party Archives.

105. Selwyn-Clarke summarized liberal concern in a widely distributed handout entitled "Tanganyika Future", released in September, 1955 FCB papers.

106. Notes in Nicholson's handwriting on FCB delegation to Lennox-Boyd, April 6, 1955, FCB papers.

107. Labour Party list of petitions and delegations to the Colonial Office involving the East and Central African dependencies, December, 1955, Labour Party Archives.

108. This strategy is detailed in the correspondence between Selwyn-Clarke and Griffiths, April 6, September 3, 1956, FCB papers.

109. Selwyn-Clarke to Creech-Jones, October 8, 1956, Creech-Jones papers.

110. Mackenzie to Selwyn-Clarke, October 29, 1956, FCB papers.

111. Nicholson-Lennox-Boyd correspondence, October 30-November 5, 1956, FCB papers.

112. Nyerere to Betts, November 7, 1956, FCB papers.

113. "Resolution of the December 8-9, 1956 Buscot Conference on Franchise and Representation in East and Central Africa," FCB papers.

114. Ibid., p. 3.

115. Nyerere to Nicholson, February 12, 1955, FCB papers.

116. Hynd to Selwyn-Clarke, April 4, 1955, Hynd files, Labour Party Archives.

117. Lennox-Boyd to Selwyn-Clarke, April 30, 1955; Nicholson notes on Kambona interviews, February-June, 1955, FCB papers.

118. Notes on interview with Lennox-Boyd, March 6, 1956, FCB papers.

119. See for example, Venture, Vol. 6, No. 1 (May 1956), pp. 8-9.

120. For example, both the FCB and the Africa Bureau opposed the Groundnut and the Sugar Schemes. Scott to Hinden, July 17, 1957, FCB papers.

121. Selwyn-Clarke to James Johnson, M. P., March 6, FCB papers.

122. Winchester to John Rankin, M. P., June 9, 1956, FCB papers. She noted that the issue was raised at the request of Kambona.

123. Brockway files, FCB papers.

124. Betts to Lennox-Boyd, July 6, 1956, FCB papers.

125. Selwyn-Clarke to Winchester, June 25, 1957, FCB papers.

126. Creech-Jones memorandum to Labour M.P.s entitled "United Nations Machinery for Dealing With Colonial and Trust Territories" July 11, 1955 Creech-Jones papers.

127. MacLeod notes on "Conditions in the East and Central Africa Dependencies," November, 1959, Macleod files, Institute of Commonwealth Studies, Oxford.

128. Based on TANU campaign literature located in FCB files.

129. For examples of the liberal viewpoint see: Marjorie Nicholson, Political Objectives and Developments, London: Fabian Publications Ltd., 1958, and Eirene White, What Hope for a Socialist Commonwealth? London: Faber and Faber, Ltd., 1959.

130. "List of TANU Engagements", a note in Selwyn-Clarke's handwriting, dated January 28, 1960, FCB papers.

131. See for example the Jamal article in Venture, Vol. 11, No. 1 (May 1959), 4 and essay by Heath, Venture, Vol. 11, No. 2 (June, 1959), 9; M. P. Arthur Skeffington to Selwyn-Clarke, on the liberal factions' publicity strategy, September 6, 1959, Labour Party Archives.

132. Skeffington correspondence with Nyerere and Kambona, October 1959- March 1960, FCB papers.

133. See for example FCB to Chief Kidaha Makwaia, October 4, 1956; Betts to Heath, July 30, 1959; Betts to Jamal, November 21, 1958, FCB papers.

134. Selwyn-Clarke to TANU Executive Committee, December 14, 1959, FCB papers.

135. Callahan Selwyn-Clarke correspondence, May 5-17, 1957, FCB papers.

136. Johnson-Winchester correspondence, April 16-June 21, 1959, FCB papers.

137. Notes on FCB investigations in Winchesters's handwriting, April 1960. The Bureau extensively interviewed Elections Officer Hucks to determine the degree of African comprehension as reported by returning officers. FCB papers.

138. Lennox-Boyd notes on an interview with Labour Party delegation, April 1, 1958, Conservative Party Headquarters.

139. Selwyn-Clarke to Hatch, October 26, 1958, FCB papers.

140. Nyerere to Betts, January 3, 1960, FCB papers.

141. Jamal to Selwyn-Clarke, December 21, 1959, FCB papers.

142. Selwyn-Clarke to MacLeod, August 9, 1961, FCB papers.

143. Kambona correspondence with FCB Secretary Catherine Hoskyns, March 16-April 23, FCB papers.

SOURCES CITED

Manuscript Collections

Rhodes House Africana Collection, Oxford, England
 Rhodes House is a major depository for primary research
 material concerning the British African dependencies.
 The key source utilized in this project are the papers
 of the Fabian Colonial Bureau (127 Boxes) covering all
 aspects of Socialist involvement in Tanganyika.

 Rhodes House also contains copious material devoted to
 all phases of territorial political development, including the papers of the Asian Association and the United
 Tanganyikan parties, the personal papers of numerous
 administrators in the Tanganyikan service, the writings
 of key Colonial Office personnel and the Provincial and
 District books of territorial officers.

Conservative Party Archives, Conservative Party Headquarters, London, England
 The Party headquarters maintains a fine collection of
 political position papers on key territorial issues,
 files covering the writings of Tory M.P.s active in the
 debate concerning Tanganyikan development, and newspaper
 clipping files covering party activities.

Labour Party Archives, Labour Party Headquarters, Transport
House, London, England
 The archive is a source of abundant material concerning
 the party's involvement with Tanganyika in the post-war
 period. Especially helpful are the files of the M.P.s
 who actively cooperated with the Fabians and with the
 TANU hierarchy.

Institute for Commonwealth Studies, Queen Elizabeth House,
Oxford, England
 The Institute maintains an extensive collection of
 primary source material concerning Colonial Office
 personnel influential in the formation of Crown policy
 in Tanganyika.

United Nations: Official Publications

United Nations. News (No. 15/56). April 12, 1956.

_____. Trusteeship Council. Official Records. (1946-1961).

_____. Trusteeship Council. Trusteeship Council Resolution 468 (XI), A/2150.

_____. Trusteeship Council. T/PVT 820. (August 1955).

_____. Visiting Mission to Trust Territories in East Africa. Report of the Visiting Mission to East Africa, 1948, T/218.

_____. Visiting Mission to Trust Territories in East Africa, 1954. Report on Tanganyika, 1954.

Great Britain: Official Publications

Great Britain. Colonial Office. Col. No. 193. Labour Conditions in East Africa. London: H.M.S.O., 1946.

_____. Parliament. House of Commons. Parliamentary Debates. (Hansard) 1946-1961.

_____. House of Lords. Parliamentary Debates. (Hansard) 1946-1961.

Tanganyika: Official Publications
of the Government of Tanganyika

Tanganyika. Report of the Committee on Constitutional Development. Dar es Salaam: Government Printer, 1951.

_____. Report of the 1954 Visiting Mission; Observations of the Administering Authority. Dar es Salaam: Government Printer, 1955.

_____. Constitutional Development Commission. Report of the Special Commissioner Appointed to Examine Matters Arising Out of the Report of the Committee on Constitutional Development. Dar es Salaam: Government Printer, 1953.

_____. Legislative Council. Order No. 11, 1954. Dar es Salaam: Government Printer, 1954.

BOOKS

Hailey, William Malcolm. Native Administration in the British African Territories. London: His Majesty's Stationery Office, 1950-53.

Nicholson, Marjorie. Political Objectives and Development. London: Fabian Publishing Ltd., 1958.

White, Eirene. What Hope for a Social Commonwealth? London: Faber and Faber, Ltd., 1959.

JOURNALS

Creech-Jones, Arthur. "A Labour View of British Colonial Policy." United Empire. Vol. XXXVI, No. 4 (July-August, 1945), 127-131.

_____. "British Colonial Policy with Reference to Africa." International Affairs. Vol. XXIV, No. 3 (August, 1951).

PAMPHLETS

Creech-Jones, Arthur. Labour's Colonial Policy. London: Fabian Publications Ltd., 1947.

Griffiths, James; Arthur Creech-Jones; Rita Hinden. The Way Forward. London: Fabian Publications, Ltd., 1950.

Hinden, Rita. Common Sense and Colonial Development. London: Fabian Publications Ltd., 1949.

_____. Socialists and the Empire: Five Years Work of the Fabian Colonial Bureau. London: Fabian Publications Ltd., 1946.

Labour Party. Labour Party Political Education Series. Discussion Notes No. 25. British Africa. London: Labour Party, 1960.

_____. _Policy in Africa_. London: The Africa Bureau, 1956.

Silberman, L. _Crisis in Africa_. London: Fabian Publications Ltd., 1947.

Skeffington, Arthur. _Tanganyika in Transition_. London: Fabian Commonwealth Bureau, 1960.

Tanganyika African National Union. _Election Manifesto 1960_. Dar es Salaam: Thakers, 1960.

CENTER FOR INTERNATIONAL STUDIES

ISBN Prefix 0-89680-

Africa Series

1. Collins, Harold Reeves. THE NEW ENGLISH OF THE ONITSHA
   CHAPBOOKS. 1968
   035-0   82-91528 $ 3.00*

2. Kotey, Paul F. A. DIRECTIONS IN GHANIAN LINGUISTICS:
   A Brief Survey. 1969
   036-9   82-91536 $ 2.50*

3. Weisfelder, Richard F. DEFINING NATIONAL PURPOSE IN
   LESOTHO. 1969
   037-7   82-91544 $ 3.25*

4. Bernard, Frank E. RECENT AGRICULTURAL CHANGE EAST OF
   MOUNT KENYA. 1969
   038-5   82-91551 $ 4.00*

5. Pollock, Norman H. THE STRUGGLE AGAINST SLEEPING
   SICKNESS IN NYASALAND AND NORTHERN RHODESIA,
   1900-1922. 1969
   039-3   82-91569 $ 3.00*

7. McCall, Daniel F. WOLF COURTS GIRL: The Equivalence
   of Hunting and Mating in Bushman Thought. 1970
   040-7   82-91585 $ 3.25*

10. Church, R. J. Harrison. SOME GEOGRAPHICAL ASPECTS OF
    WEST AFRICAN DEVELOPMENT. 1971
    043-1   82-91619 $ 3.50*

11. Bowie, Leland. THE IMPACT OF THE PROTEGE SYSTEM IN
    MOROCCO, 1880-1912. 1971
    044-X   82-91627 $ 2.75*

12. Good, Charles M. MARKET DEVELOPMENT IN TRADITIONALLY
    MARKETLESS SOCIETIES: A Perspective on East
    Africa. 1971
    045-8   82-91635 $ 4.00*

13. Bowman, Larry. SOUTH AFRICA'S OUTWARD STRATEGY: A
    Foreign Policy Dilemma for the United States. 1971
    046-6   82-91643 $ 3.25*

14. Davis, R. Hunt, Jr. BANTU EDUCATION AND THE EDUCATION
    OF AFRICANS IN SOUTH AFRICA. 1972
    047-4   82-91650 $ 4.50*

15. Nyquist, Thomas E. TOWARD A THEORY OF THE AFRICAN UPPER
        STRATUM IN SOUTH AFRICA. 1972
        048-2   82-91668 $ 4.50*

16. Weisfelder, Richard F. THE BASOTHO MONARCHY: A Spent
        Force or a Dynamic Political Factor? 1972
        049-0   82-91676 $ 7.00*

18. Strate, Jeffrey T. POST-MILITARY COUP STRATEGY IN
        UGANDA: Amin's Early Attempts to Consolidate
        Political Support. 1973
        051-2   82-91692 $ 4.50*

19. Huntsberger, Paul E., compiler. HIGHLAND MOSAIC: A
        Critical Anthology of Ethiopian Literature in
        English. 1973
        052-0   82-91718 $ 7.00*

20. Coe, Richard L. THE KENYA NATIONAL YOUTH SERVICE: A
        Governmental Response to Young Political Activists.
        1973
        053-9   82-91718 $ 4.00*

21. Silberfein, Marilyn. CONSTRAINTS ON THE EXPANSION OF
        COMMERCIAL AGRICULTURE: Iringa District, Tanzania.
        1974
        054-7   82-91726 $ 4.50*

22. Pieterse, Cosmo. ECHO AND CHORUSES: "Ballad of the
        Cells" and Selected Shorter Poems. 1974
        055-5   82-91734 $ 5.00*

23. Thom, Derrick J. THE NIGER-NIGERIA BOUNDARY: A Study
        of Ethnic Frontiers and a Colonial Boundary. 1975
        056-3   82-91742 $ 4.75*

24. Baum, Edward, compiler. A COMPREHENSIVE PERIODICAL
        BIBLIOGRAPHY OF NIGERIA, 1960-1970. 1975
        057-1   82-91759 $13.00*

25. Kirchherr, Eugene C. ABYSSINIA TO ZIMBABWE: A Guide
        to the Political Units of Africa in the Period
        1947-1978. 1979, 3rd edition
        100-4   82-91908 $ 8.00*

26. Nair, Kannan K. THE ORIGINS AND DEVELOPMENT OF EFIK
        SETTLEMENTS IN SOUTHEASTERN NIGERIA. 1976
        059-8   82-91775 $ 4.00*

27. Fadiman, Jeffrey A. MOUNTAIN WARRIORS: The Pre-Colonial
        Meru of Mt. Kenya. 1976
        060-1   82-91783 $ 4.75*

29. Baum, Edward and Felix Gagliano. CHIEF EXECUTIVES IN
    BLACK AFRICA AND SOUTHEAST ASIA: A Descriptive
    Analysis of Social Background Characteristics. 1976
    025-3   82-91809 $ 4.00*

30. Samaan, Sadek H. and Anne J. Samaan. FEARS AND WORRIES
    OF NIGERIAN IGBO SECONDARY SCHOOL STUDENTS: An
    Empirical Psycho-cultural Study. 1976
    062-8   82-91817 $ 6.00*

32. Wright, Donald R. THE EARLY HISTORY OF THE NIUMI:
    Settlement and Foundation of a Mandinka State on
    the Gambia River. 1977
    064-4   82-91833 $ 8.00*

33. Grundy, Kenneth W. DEFENSE LEGISLATION AND COMMUNAL
    POLITICS: The Evolution of a White South African
    Nation as Reflected in the Controversy over the
    Assignment of Armed Forces Abroad, 1912-1976. 1978
    065-2   82-91841 $ 5.00*

34. Clayton, Anthony. COMMUNICATIONS FOR NEW LOYALTIES:
    African Soldiers' Songs. 1978
    069-5   82-91858 $ 6.00*

35. duToit, Brian M. DRUG USE AND SOUTH AFRICAN STUDENTS.
    1978
    076-8   82-91866 $ 7.50*

36. Fadiman, Jeffrey A. THE MOMENT OF CONQUEST: Meru, Kenya,
    1907. 1979
    081-4   82-91874 $ 5.50*

37. Wright, Donald R. ORAL TRADITIONS FROM THE GAMBIA:
    Volume I, Mandinka Griots. 1979
    083-0   82-91882 $12.00*

38. Wright, Donald R. ORAL TRADITIONS FROM THE GAMBIA:
    Volume II, Family Elders. 1980
    084-9   82-91890 $15.00*

39. Reining, Priscilla. CHALLENGING DESERTIFICATION IN WEST
    AFRICA: Insights from Landsat into Carrying
    Capacity, Cultivation and Settlement Site
    Indentification in Upper Volta and Niger. 1979
    102-0   82-91916 $12.00*

41. Lindfors, Bernth. MAZUNGUMZO: Interviews with East
    African Writers, Publishers, Editors and Scholars.
    1981
    108-X   82-91932 $13.00*

42. Spear, Thomas J. TRADITIONS OF ORIGIN AND THEIR
    INTERPRETATION: The Mijikenda of Kenya. 1982
    109-8   82-91940 $13.50*

43. Harik, Elsa and Donald Schilling. THE POLITICS OF
    EDUCATION IN COLONIAL ALGERIA AND KENYA. 1984
    117-9   82-91957 $11.50*

Latin America Series

1. Frei M., Eduardo. THE MANDATE OF HISTORY AND CHILE'S
   FUTURE. 1977
   066-0   82-92526 $ 8.00*

2. Irish, Donald P., ed. MULTINATIONAL CORPORATIONS IN
   LATIN AMERICA: Private Rights -- Public
   Responsibilities. 1978
   067-9   82-92534 $ 9.00*

3. Molineu, Harold, ed. MULTINATIONAL CORPORATIONS AND
   INTERNATIONAL INVESTMENTS IN LATIN AMERICA: A
   Selected Bibliography. 1978
   068-7   82-92542 $ 9.00*

4. Martz, Mary Jeanne Reid. THE CENTRAL AMERICAN SOCCER
   WAR: Historical Patterns and Internal Dynamics of
   OAS Settlement Procedures. 1979
   077-6   82-92559 $ 8.00*

5. Wiarda, Howard J. CRITICAL ELECTIONS AND CRITICAL COUPS:
   State, Society, and the Military in the Processes
   of Latin American Development. 1979
   082-2   82-92567 $ 7.00*

6. Dietz, Henry A. and Richard Moore. POLITICAL PARTICI-
   PATION IN A NON-ELECTORAL SETTING: The Urban Poor
   in Lima, Peru. 1979
   085-7   82-92575 $ 9.00*

7. Hopgood, James F. SETTLERS OF BAJAVISTA: Social and
   Economic Adaptation in a Mexican Squatter Settlement. 1979
   101-2   82-92583 $11.00*

8. Clayton, Lawrence A. CAULKERS AND CARPENTERS IN A NEW
   WORLD: The Shipyards of Colonial Guayaquil. 1980
   103-9   82-92591 $15.00*

9. Tata, Robert J. STRUCTURAL CHANGES IN PUERTO RICO'S
   ECONOMY: 1947-1976. 1981
   107-1   82-92609 $11.75*

10. McCreery, David. DEVELOPMENT AND THE STATE IN REFORMA
       GUATEMALA. 1983
       113-6   82-92617 $ 8.50*

Southeast Asia Series

11. Aun, Tan Sri Lim Swee. RUBBER AND THE MALAYSIAN
       ECONOMY: Implications of Declining Prices. 1969
       005-9   82-90124 $ 4.00*

18. Suryadinata, Leo. THE PRE-WORLD WAR II PERANAKAN CHINESE
       PRESS OF JAVA: A Preliminary Survey. 1971
       011-3   82-90199 $ 4.00*

26. van der Veur, Paul and Lian The, compilers. THE
       VERHANDELINGEN VAN HET BATAVIAASCH GENOOTSCHAP:
       An Annotated Content Analysis. 1973
       014-8   82-90272 $10.00*

31. Nash, Manning. PEASANT CITIZENS: Politics, Religion,
       and Modernization in Kelantan, Malaysia. 1974
       018-0   82-90322 $12.00*

32. de Queljoe, David. MARGINAL MAN IN COLONIAL SOCIETY:
       Abdoel Moeis' Salah Asuhan. 1974
       019-9   82-90330 $ 4.00*

34. Callison, C. Stuart. THE LAND-TO-THE-TILLER PROGRAM AND
       RURAL RESOURCE MOBILIZATION IN THE MEKONG DELTA OF
       SOUTH VIETNAM. 1974
       020-9   82-90355 $ 4.50*

36. Poole, Peter A., ed. INDOCHINA: Perspectives for
       Reconciliation. 1976
       022-9   82-90371 $ 6.00*

38. Bailey, Conner. BROKER, MEDIATOR, PATRON, AND KINSMAN:
       An Historical Analysis of Key Leadership Roles in
       a Rural Malaysian District. 1976
       024-5   82-90397 $ 7.00*

39. Baum, Edward and Felix Gagliano. CHIEF EXECUTIVES IN
       BLACK AFRICA AND SOUTHEAST ASIA: A Descriptive
       Analysis of Social Background Characteristics. 1976
       025-3   82-90405 $ 4.00*

40. van der Veur, Paul W. FREEMASONRY IN INDONESIA FROM
       RADERMACHER TO SOEKANTO, 1762-1961. 1976
       026-1   82-90413 $ 4.00*

43. Marlay, Ross. POLLUTION AND POLITICS IN THE PHILIPPINES.
      1977
      029-6   82-90447 $ 7.00*

44. Collier, William L., et. al. INCOME, EMPLOYMENT AND FOOD
      SYSTEMS IN JAVANESE COASTAL VILLAGES. 1977
      031-8   82-90454 $10.00*

45. Foon, Chew Sock and John A. MacDougall. FOREVER PLURAL:
      The Perception and Practice of Inter-communal
      Marriage in Singapore. 1977
      030-X   82-90462 $ 6.00*

46. Bradley, William, et. al. THAILAND, DOMINO BY DEFAULT?
      The 1976 Coup and Implications for U.S. Policy.
      With an epilogue on the 1977 Coup. 1978
      032-6   82-90470 $ 6.00*

47. Wessing, Robert. COSMOLOGY AND SOCIAL BEHAVIOR IN A
      WEST JAVANESE SETTLEMENT. 1978
      072-5   82-90488 $12.00*

48. Willer, Thomas F., ed. SOUTHEAST ASIAN REFERENCES IN THE
      BRITISH PARLIAMENTARY PAPERS, 1801-1972/73: An
      Index. 1977
      033-4   82-90496 $ 8.50*

49. Durrenberger, E. Paul. AGRICULTURAL PRODUCTION AND
      HOUSEHOLD BUDGETS IN A SHAN PEASANT VILLAGE IN
      NORTHWESTERN THAILAND: A Quantitative Description.
      1978
      071-7   82-90504 $ 9.50*

50. Echauz, Robustiano. SKETCHES OF THE ISLAND OF NEGROS.
      1978.
      070-9   82-90512 $10.00*

51. Krannich, Ronald L. MAYORS AND MANAGERS IN THAILAND:
      The Struggle for Political Life in Administrative
      Settings. 1978
      073-3   82-90520 $ 9.00*

52. Davis, Gloria, ed. WHAT IS MODERN INDONESIAN CULTURE?
      1978
      075-X   82-90538 $18.00*

53. Bruner, Edward M. and Judith A. Becker, eds. ART, RITUAL
      AND SOCIETY IN INDONESIA. 1979
      080-6   82-90546 $13.00*

54. Ayal, Eliezar B., ed. THE STUDY OF THAILAND: Anaylses of Knowledge, Approaches, and Prospects in Anthropology, Art History, Economics, History and Political Science. 1979
079-2   82-90553 $13.50*

55. Smyser, W. R. THE INDEPENDENT VIETNAMESE: Vietnamese Communism Between Russia and China, 1956-1969. 1980
105-5   82-90561 $12.75*

56. Duiker, William J. VIETNAM SINCE THE FALL OF SAIGON. 1981
106-3   82-90579 $ 9.00*

57. Siregar, Susan Rodgers. ADAT, ISLAM, AND CHRISTIANITY IN A BATAK HOMELAND. 1981
110-1   82-90587 $10.00*

58. Van Esterik, Penny. COGNITION AND DESIGN PRODUCTION IN BAN CHIANG POTTERY. 1981
078-4   82-90595 $12.00*

59. Foster, Brian L. COMMERCE AND ETHNIC DIFFERENCES: The Case of the Mons in Thailand. 1982
112-8   82-90603 $10.00*

60. Frederick, William H. and John H. McGlynn. REFLECTIONS ON REBELLION: Stories from the Indonesian Upheavals of 1948 and 1965. 1983
111-X   82-90611 $ 9.00*

61. Cady, John F. CONTACTS WITH BURMA, 1935-1949: A Personal Account. 1983
114-4   82-90629 $ 9.00*

62. Kipp, Rita Smith and Richard D. Kipp, eds. BEYOND SAMOSIR: Recent Studies of the Batak Peoples of Sumatra. 1983
115-2   82-90637 $ 9.00*

63. Carstens, Sharon, ed. CULTURAL IDENTITY IN NORTHERN PENINSULAR MALAYSIA.
116-0   82-90637   forthcoming

64. Dardjowidjojo, Soenjono. VOCABULARY BUILDING IN INDONESIAN: An Advanced Reader. 1984
118-7   82-90652 $18.00*t

65. Errington, J. Joseph. LANGUAGE AND SOCIAL CHANGE IN JAVA: Linguistic Reflexes of Modernization in a Traditional Royal Polity. 1984
120-9   82-90660 $12.00*t

66. Binh, Tran Bu. Translated by John Spragens. THE RED EARTH: A Vietnamese Memoir of Life on a Colonial Rubber Plantation. 1984
119-5   82-90678 $ 9.00*t

67. Pane, Armijn. Translated by John McGlynn. Introduction by William H. Frederick. SHACKLES. 1984
122-5   82-90686 $ 9.00*t

68. Syukri, Ibrahim. Translated by Conner Bailey and John N. Miksic. Introduction by David Wyatt. SEJARAH KERAJAAN MELAYU PATANI: A History of the Malay Kingdom of Patani.
122-3   82-90694   forthcoming

69. Keeler, Ward. JAVANESE: A Cultural Approach. 1984
121-7   82-90702 $18.00*

t indicates a tentative price

ORDERING INFORMATION

Orders for titles in the Monographs in International Studies series should be placed through Ohio University Press/ Scott Quadrangle/Athens, Ohio, 45701. Individuals must remit prepayment via check, VISA, MasterCard, CHOICE or American Express. Individuals ordering from outside of the U.S. please remit in U.S. funds by either International Money Order or check drawn on a U.S. bank. Residents of Ohio and Missouri please add applicable sales tax. Postage and handling is $2.00 for the first book and 50¢ for each additional book. Prices and availability are subject to change without notice.